Freelance Fancy

Your Guide to
Capturing
Spiritual Health,
Wealth
and Happiness
from Gig Work

By Sherry Beck Paprocki

Although every precaution has been taken in the
preparation of this book, the author assumes no
responsibility for errors or omissions. Neither is any
liability assumed for damages resulting from the
use of information contained herein. For information,
contact: R.S. Rock Media, Inc., 8888 Grate Park Sq.,
New Albany, OH 43054.

www.rsrock.media

ISBN 978-0-9963065-2-2

Cover design by Betsy Becker
with assistance from Van-garde.com

Interior design and layout by Van-garde.com

Library of Congress Cataloging-in Publication Data

Paprocki, Sherry Beck
[Freelance Fancy: Your Guide to Capturing
Spiritual Health, Wealth and Happiness from Gig Work]

(electronic/multiple format –
ISBN 978-0-9963065-3-9 (electronic/epub)
1. Nonfiction—Business
2. Self-perception
3. Freelance
4. Paprocki, Sherry Beck

Table of Contents

This book is dedicated to:

My grandmothers Frances Kowalski Dundr
and Myra Worthington Beck,
my mother Nancy Beck,
and the many other women who came
before me, who chose to do gig work
that wrapped around their own families.

And also to:
Benjamin, Griffin and Libby

Without these three people, this book
would not have been written.

Acknowledgements

Thank you to Ray Paprocki,
Justin Paprocki and Ana Paprocki Piper
for the patience that you've displayed throughout
my gig career.

Ross Beck, with much gratitude for granting
me an entrepreneurial mindset.

Special thanks to the gifted writers
who offered Wise Words of advice for this book:

Andrea King Collier

Jack El-Hai

Estelle Erasmus

Sandra Gurvis

Christopher Johnston

Janine Latus

JoBeth McDaniel

Mary Mihaly

Michelle Rafter

Introduction

MORE THAN 30 YEARS ago I decided to freelance because I needed a job that wrapped around my young family. In other words, I wanted to spend more time with my kids and less time on my work. I strived for flexibility in my workday and freedom in the work I chose to do.

As a writer, editor and an enthusiast for the powers of creation, I am sharing the lessons I've learned with you and others who seek nontraditional work—whether you are starting out in your gig career, learning to juggle family and work life, or careening into retirement as someone who balances multiple gigs to keep the cash flowing. I hope that this book will provide you with the tools and inspiration you need to design the best career possible. I am especially grateful that several of my busy freelance colleagues have agreed to add their own special words of advice here, too.

This story is my attempt to share the magic—as well as the madness—that goes on behind the curtains in the life of a prolific freelancer. I promise that the lessons we've learned will not only help you build your own gig career, but they will also lead you on a pathway toward the financial and spiritual rewards that everyone deserves.

This book is divided into six sections addressing your entrepreneurial spirit, your freelance mindset, following a greater purpose, inspiration and passion, perspective, and leadership.

In Part I we'll discuss your entrepreneurial spirit and how successful freelancers have many of the same characteristics as successful entrepreneurs. They take risks, they love exploring new ideas and they quickly pivot.

Part II stresses the importance of learning the basic freelance mindset you'll need to do gig work before you jump in. But more than that, this section also addresses the PPR of building a freelance business: understanding the *people* who buy your work, knowing that there will be *problems*, and recognizing the importance of *relationships*.

Once you get to Part III, you'll begin to see how your work can lead you toward a greater purpose. Finding a niche that excites you and understanding the appropriate methods of communicating stories in that niche are important lessons to learn.

In Part IV, you'll read how passion and determination will lead you to career success. I share how gaining perspective on my freelance work after many years helped me figure out what was next in my life. I was teaching a room overflowing with freelance writers the importance of a person's gravity well when I finally began to understand the act of reflection and how it's imperative to, at times, realign your spirit with your career goals.

In Part V, you'll read about how your career will be challenged through difficult economic periods and how it will survive when you are unafraid of the risks associated with disruption. (I hope you even experience some of the sweaty-palmed excitement I've had when I've taken big risks.)

Part VI will address various facets of leadership. Ultimately, perhaps, we talk about ego, which teeters near the top of Maslow's Pyramid. As you finish, you'll better understand your own ego before we start tackling the difficult task of gaining spiritual health and life balance as you work toward the greater good of society.

Throughout this book, you'll meet many people who have influenced my career and my life. Often those influences came from the people I was interviewing and researching for articles and books. But I have also been heavily influenced by the dozens of writers I know, as well as other successful creatives who have toiled away on their passions to build big companies, dream up amazing nonprofits, and use their lives' work to impact the greater good.

These lessons took years for me to learn and were the result of thousands of interviews, hours of research and plenty of mistakes made along the way. In his book

Outliers, author Malcolm Gladwell talks about gaining 10,000 hours of experience to become the ultimate professional in any career field. I completely agree. There is nothing that replaces career experience. Certainly, there are no shortcuts to a writing career.

But if I help you have a smarter freelance career sooner than I did, then I've accomplished my purpose. At heart, I'm a writer, a journalist and an editor. But I've had more gigs—both in my chosen field and outside of it—than I care to count, including being a publisher, as well as a fit model in my 50s for a national retail brand that was launching a petite line of clothing.

My freelance career has taken thousands of twists and turns in more than three decades of work. I've written for big city newspapers and important magazines. I've penned more than a dozen books and created fiction for a literary app. I've written white papers and ghost-written memoirs.

Many times, I interviewed people in their homes and sometimes I have interviewed them about their homes. Through the years, I have reported on the lifestyles of hundreds of successful people who are quietly wealthy. They aren't celebrities who get constant attention, but they are powerful people who—in some cases—create political change.

Finally, I am unapologetic when I tell you that I have a degree in journalism and that has shaped my viewpoint of the world. I'm continuously motivated to protect the fragile American privilege of a free press and free speech. I am enthralled with the politics of our country, and I will continue to speak out to protect our country's First Amendment rights.

From 2016 to 2018, I was president of the American Society of Journalists and Authors, the biggest organization in the U.S.—and quite possibly the world—comprised of independent nonfiction writers. This volunteer gig informed me of so much more.

First it informed me even more about the awesome economic power in gig work. In an economy that fluctuates between good times and bad, gig workers in this country can be big earners. Two freelance tech writers on the west coast told me that their earnings amounted to $250,000, each, in one year. Plenty of other freelancers have shared that their earnings soar well into the six figures with the opportunities that exist for gig writers in today's digitized environment. In fact, I've experienced my own six-figure years. Just recently, I did a tally to realize that I've earned at least $2 million during my gig career.

Freelancers today are a major force in the U.S. economy. According to a 2019 study by the Freelancers Union and Upwork, 57 million people in the U.S. did some sort of freelance work in 2019. Our work amounted to more than a billion hours in that year and a contribution of more than $1 trillion toward the U.S. economy. That's a bigger contribution than several other industries including construction and transportation.

Things have changed since 2019, though. There's a growing trend of freelancers among all generations. Twenty-nine percent of baby boomers say they have freelanced, 31 percent of GenXers say they've freelanced, 40 percent of millennials have freelanced, and 53 percent of GenZers have freelanced.

Those numbers are about to grow. A survey done by Upwork in 2021 found that 10 million employees were considering turning to freelance careers. The challenges of Covid-19 coupled with the pandemic-related remote workplace have led to an avalanche of workers who are seriously looking into the benefits of being part of the gig economy.

"With a strengthening labor market, we will increasingly see people work on the terms that they prefer, and for many that means freelancing," said Adam Ozimek, Upwork's chief economist.

What follows is a story centered on my own gig work. You'll notice that my story is embedded in the context of my family life, because it's the people in your life—your partner, your children, your colleagues, other family and friends—who will be your support system and your driving force throughout your career.

Part I:

Discover Your Entrepreneurial Spirit

1. Risk-taking is Required

Adventure is inherent in my soul. As I've come to know freelancers around the country, many have similar traits. We like new challenges and push ourselves hard to work at new experiences. Each week we tackle new topics, frequently collaborating with new bosses and clients. We persevere through difficult challenges and, despite being highly competitive, we gain support from our hive of peers. We freelance workers are the gold rush diggers of the new millennia, exploring the vast digital terrain that continually demands new content.

When I was a teenager, no one knew the digital frontier was approaching. No one knew that eventually the quest for fresh digital content would be insatiable leading to lucrative writing gigs offered not only by prestigious publications, but also by the biggest corporations and nonprofits. We skated on a rather different, unique terrain.

The strip pits in eastern Ohio are open valleys in the hills that had been dug out by monolithic coal mining shovels with names such as the Silver Spade and the Gem of Egypt. The purpose of these huge coal shovels, which dwarfed the biggest bulldozers you've ever seen, was to scoop out the dirt that covered the coal seams that stretched through Ohio's Appalachian foothills.

In the height of winter, I would climb a barbed wire fence with my friends, so that we could ice skate on an isolated and rather eerie frozen pond settled into the bottom of a strip pit. Rough terrain and rocky cliffs surrounded us, offering a mystical winter site that set the stage for a spectacular skating experience.

As dusk fell during one of those trips, my friends and I climbed back over the fence to meet our ride home. As I climbed, the rusty barbed wire had clenched the inner seam of my first and only pair of blue jeans. A spike from the wire grabbed hold of the denim in a death grip that stopped me from finishing my climb and incapacitated me from sitting down on the unstable wire, for fear that a spiky point would plunge deep into my inner thigh. I carefully balanced there, two gloved hands clenching the top wire, lifting my rear off it.

"I'm stuck. Help!" I called out to my friends.

My friend Sharon ran to my rescue. It was cold and

not yet funny, as it would become in later years, but she pulled her mitten from her hand, worked her fingers along the fence and freed me. We all then rushed out of the woods toward the car where my friend Joyce's stepdad awaited us.

Later, I cut off the bottoms of those jeans, patched the tear in them and stitched them into a purse with a strap. And then, a few years after that in the era of short shorts, I clipped the seams I'd sewn and wore them once again as shorts.

Looking back, that pair of jeans says something about a characteristic I've seen in many freelancers. It's about being resourceful. It's about taking one topic and spinning it out into several different directions. It's about gaining basic knowledge that can be the building blocks for a whole career.

My strip pit skating experience taught me three things: I enjoy taking risks, it's always important to have a hive of friends and any new experience can spark ideas.

A freelance writer's days are filled with research, interviewing sources and writing stories about various topics. What I learned through the years was that the more often I could write about the same topic, the more I could earn. Tackling a fresh topic, as many writers found with Covid-19 in 2020, requires hours and hours of research. Many of the health writers I know mastered the topic and spun it off to three or four publications each week with a different spin on each story. They were practicing smart business and we were all better informed because of it.

Finding a hive of peers is an important aspect of freelancing, and bonding with other giggers will determine your success. Freelancers are the solopreneurs of the world who spend much time alone, at their desks. You should be proactive in gathering with others who practice your craft, though.

When I was a new freelancer, I gathered locally for informal coffees with other freelancers. I even joined a freelance friend and launched an annual writers' conference that was quite successful during the 10 years that we ran it.

Indeed, those local liaisons were healthy for me at the time and helped launch my author career. I've found, though, that there will be plenty of times in your life that you'll reach for more. To guide your entrepreneurial spirit, you'll search for more people who will continue to inspire you.

It was for that reason that I began attending conferences in bigger cities, among them Chicago and New York. I met many other people who were just like me. Some had degrees from top universities for journalism, and we quickly bonded. Eventually, I paid what seemed to be a steep fee and applied for membership into the American Society of Journalists and Authors. The friends and mentors I had once I joined ASJA magnified my freelance career and helped me see the possibilities beyond.

Freelancers are really the unicorns of the world. If you talk to six successful freelancers, you'll find that each and every one of them has followed a unique career path. When you're sitting in on a virtual conference in Los Angeles or you're in a hotel meeting room in New York, you'll hear an idea that will spur you into action. That's how big careers get built. Never, ever think that people build big freelance careers by sitting in rooms off by themselves all day long. Inspiration comes with special experiences.

One of the best ways to immerse yourself in a freelance life is to attend those big meetings, and then put together smaller groups of like-minded people during those events to form long-lasting friendships that will build your career. We writers have spent many cozy evenings at restaurants and hotels across the country, eating dinners and sipping wine as we discussed our shared challenges, our recent successes, our frustrations and our goals for the future. There is no digital forum, including Facebook, Instagram, Snapchat, TikTok and others, that can replace the face-to-face connection that will bond you with your peers.

As your career and the careers of those in your hive grow, you'll learn from each other the pitfalls to avoid and the frustrations to eliminate. But more than that, you'll find that doors open to new work because you get recommendations. Jobs are given to you because another gigger is too busy, and lifestyles become apparent to you because someone else has designed their worklife with balance and forethought.

The conversations that you have will spark new ideas that you will incorporate into your career path. Once your mind is open to the fact that anyone and any experience can spark an idea, you'll be driven to collect more unique experiences that will influence your creative work.

You will be so invigorated by all the ideas in the world, that your passion for creativity and innovation will spill over into all parts of your life. Your desire for creative experiences will pull you away from a computer screen. You may spend more time in nature being awed by your surroundings. You may find that you're more adventuresome. You may take up new hobbies and try unusual vacations. All of this will feed your career.

Then, your enthusiasm for your work life will spill over and affect others. You'll inspire your friends and your family. As your career evolves, you'll clear new pathways and encourage others to do so, too. We're getting ahead of ourselves here, but I think you know what

I mean. The mental engagement that you put into a freelance career will, in the long term, affect so much of your life that you'll want others to experience it, too.

Shortcut to Success:

Before you launch a serious freelance career, consider whether you have some of the entrepreneurial qualities listed below:

- Do you enjoy taking risks?
- Do you have more ideas than most people?
- Do you like to promote your work and get new clients?
- Do you get joy out of working with a hive of peers?
- Are you capable of juggling multiple tasks in one day?
- Do you have a vision of where you'd like for your business to be in five or 10 years?

2. Family Matters

"Work hard, but don't talk about your achievements and certainly don't elevate yourself above anyone else." That was the message my three sisters and I received as we emerged into young women.

Throughout my life people have asked questions about my freelance writing career. Questions come from doctors, lawyers, teachers, journalists and plenty of new college graduates who are trying to figure out their own career paths.

As my career progressed, this was a stumbling block for me. It's difficult to talk about your achievements, without feeling as though you are boasting. Eventually, though, I realized that I needed to talk more about my work so that I could mentor others. That's one reason why I decided to write this book.

In college, I learned about the late psychologist Abraham Maslow's Hierarchy of Needs. That helped me gain perspective. Diagrammed in a pyramid, Maslow believed that a person must feel that their basic needs are met involving water, food, warmth, rest, safety and security before they can truly accomplish anything else in life. If those first two levels of the pyramid are not met, then that person will struggle to get to a higher level of living.

Maslow's Pyramid

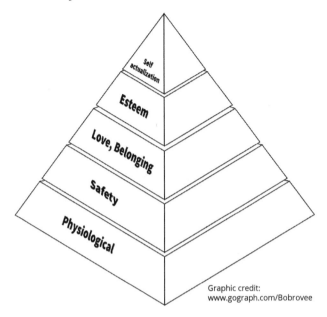

Graphic credit:
www.gograph.com/Bobrovee

Maslow's third level is social. That's where I learned that a sense of community and intimacy among family and friends is necessary for a good life. From church groups to high school skating parties, my social life was always big and fulfilling. So fulfilling, in fact, that as a teenager my mother often admonished me for not paying closer attention to my studies.

There's another aspect to social life that I want to address here, too. Choosing the right partner has made my career life much easier. Being a freelancer meant that I would be on constant deadlines and paychecks would be sporadic. It takes a special person to understand the pressures of a gig lifestyle. The need for understanding is compounded if you are rearing children together.

It's imperative that your partner supports your work.

It probably won't take you years to determine if someone is right for you, you'll know pretty quickly. Why? Because being with that person should seem easy.

My list of how to choose any partner is a short one: Choose someone who understands your passions, shares a similar intellect and curiosity, and listens to every word you say as you are dating. Choose a person you are sure you can trust, someone who respects your thoughts, who appreciates your friends and family and, finally, choose someone who knows how to celebrate your successes. A sense of humor is helpful, too.

Our chatter was incessant, light and fun. Ray and I laughed as we danced *La La Land*-style across the campus of Ohio State University that summer evening soon after we'd met. He held our clasped hands high, and I spun underneath.

"Where would you go if you could go anywhere in the world?" he asked me.

"I have no idea," I responded. Our destination that evening was a romantic spot called Mirror Lake. "There are so many places in this country that I would still like to visit, I haven't thought much beyond that."

Ray's father was an airline mechanic and, at the time I met him, Ray had a free ticket to travel anywhere in the world. Although we both came from blue collar backgrounds, by this time Ray was privileged to have traveled halfway around the globe. He knew the United States and its airports like most people know their own hometowns. I was fascinated by his stories of traveling to exotic places.

"Yes, I've been to the Vatican and I've seen the Pope," he explained one day during a conversation about his travels. "I was with my father, mother and grandmother. The Pope saw me in the crowd and blessed me with the sign of the cross."

Ray also read newspapers from throughout the United States. His Dad brought them home from the airport every day.

Ray and I met in the newsroom of the college's daily newspaper where journalism students sharpen their skills. While I was the lone student reporter covering the Ohio legislature, fittingly to his life's experiences, Ray was aiming to be the wire editor at *The Lantern*, where he would read the global stories coming in from the Associated Press and decide which would be printed in the school newspaper.

Together that spring, we wrote one article about the

day that two presidential candidates showed up in Columbus. It was 1980. Ray covered Ronald Reagan on the lawn of the Ohio Statehouse while I covered Jimmy Carter's appearance on the other side of Downtown Columbus. We each wrote paragraphs related to our guy's event, and after we filed our story, we went out for drinks. Later, Ronald Reagan won the race.

I liked Ray's easygoing demeanor and unique viewpoint of the world.

During the summer we dated, he was painting houses to earn money for his apartment rent as well as working a part-time gig at a local newspaper. Throughout college, I held numerous part-time jobs to pay for my own food and rent. Our industrious lifestyles and adventuresome mindsets seemed well matched. We were married before the year ended.

❧

If you study Maslow's Pyramid—or revisit it—it will likely make a lot of sense to you. Once the basic needs are fulfilled, then a person may better focus on establishing a sense of accomplishment. Whether that's in a career or in a social setting, people who do not struggle with meeting their basic needs will have the time and mindfulness to advance their role into one that better serves the community as a whole.

Many people have difficulty making it to the top

level of Maslow's Pyramid—the self-actualization level. This is when you are respected by your peers, and you receive the accolades that you deserve. This is a level where you begin feeling like you have fulfilled your life's mission.

Without really thinking too much about it, Maslow's Pyramid became a map for my life.

Shortcut to Success:

Consider Maslow's Pyramid and be sure that your basic needs are met before you launch a freelance career. Freelance writing will require a lot of brainpower. Before you commit, ask yourself these questions:

- Do you have enough savings to feed, clothe and house yourself for three to six months while you launch your career?

- Is failure an option for you?

- Freelance earnings ebb and flow. How will you support yourself when earnings are low?

3. Have Resilience

In your career and in your life, it is important to be resilient. Expect challenges. When a challenge occurs, don't freak out. Instead, immediately devise a plan to manage it. I learned the lesson of resilience when, at age 23, I became a mom.

Having a baby early in my twenties never seemed to be an obstacle. Both Ray and I worked hard to juggle time with our son, Justin, as well as focus on each of our careers. We were fortunate to be in a profession that seemed to proliferate with gigs.

I became a freelance reporter for a Washington, D.C. news service, again covering the Ohio legislature as I had done as a college student working for the school newspaper. Already, I was acquainted with the legislators, most of them men, including former GOP presidential hopeful John Kasich and U.S. Sen. Sherrod Brown, who currently chairs the important Senate Committee on Banking, Housing and Urban Affairs. Those two guys were the youngest in the Ohio legislature at that time.

I liked the work summarizing newly proposed laws and I was invigorated by the policy discussions that I witnessed on the legislative floors. There was an added advantage: I only needed a babysitter a couple of afternoons each week while I attended those legislative sessions. The downfall: I only received a paycheck on the weeks that the legislature was in session.

Oftentimes, though, one gig attracts others. During the time I worked at the Statehouse, an older female reporter asked if I would be her clip service and encouraged me to take six-month-old Justin to a downtown office, where I'd spend the morning, sitting on the floor while I clipped her stories from newspapers while Justin sat next to me, big blue eyes wide open for our coworking adventure. Between my two gigs and Ray's own freelance work we were able to balance our budget.

Despite our attraction to larger cities—New York or Washington, D.C.—we knew that living there would be expensive and uncomfortable while we reared our son. Eventually we searched for full-time work in Columbus and cities that were much smaller. That's how we landed in the mountain town of Beckley, West Virginia.

There, I took a position as a health and education reporter and Ray wrote about business and the arts as a freelancer. When I returned home from the newspaper every afternoon around 4 p.m., he would leave to do his own reporting at a desk at the newspaper's office while I had dinner with Justin, entertained him throughout the evening and settled him into bed.

I loved my daily reporting tasks, working regularly with educators in the local school district and physicians at several local hospitals. A highlight of those reporting days involved covering an intubation done by Dr. Henry Heimlich, the inventor of the Heimlich Maneuver. As Dr. Heimlich shoved a tube through the neck of a woman with lung disease, my head spun and I nearly dropped to the floor, unable to catch my breath. I was saved from this embarrassment only by the nurses who escorted me out of surgery into a space with more fresh air.

During the evenings, Ray took his freelance work seriously. So seriously, in fact, that the executive editor required him to cut back after he busted the budget for freelancers the first month we were there. Ray's early experience with this freelance gig formed a long-term understanding of the hard work that would involve my upcoming career.

Shortcut to Success:

Being resilient so that you can easily make change is an important attribute of a freelance writer. Freelancers often move quickly from one topic to the next. They may work with three different clients, or more, in one day. When a life-altering event occurs, such as it did with the Covid-19 pandemic, freelance writers are able to quickly pivot, dropping everything to change course.

4. Know Your Strengths

I learned a difficult lesson while working in Beckley. Not everyone is cut out to do certain jobs. You may have the skills necessary, but in your heart, you'll know the career path isn't for you. If a metaphorical door is too difficult to break through, go another direction.

If a job doesn't feel like the right fit for you, it's time to do something else. If a client is too difficult, then they are not the right client. If a gig feels too far afield, then say "no thank you" when it's offered. Trust that by saying "no," another job offer will likely soon follow.

People spend a lot of energy trying to start businesses, write books, create professional alliances and be successful. Sometimes that success eludes them. If that's the case for you, then reconsider. Don't waste another minute knocking on a locked door that won't open.

During my career, I've had many such experiences. There were book proposals that didn't get purchased, magazine articles that went unsold, essays that were rejected. Freelance writers are nothing without the persistence to continually publish. I've found, though, sometimes the doors that open the easiest are the best parts of your journey.

There's an important lesson in all of this. Before you start your freelance career, try to figure out your strengths. What are the projects that inspire you? What are you most curious about? What are your biggest skills and gifts? What do people repeatedly compliment you about regarding your skill set?

Somehow, I knew my full-time work as a reporter and editor would be cut short. I had a burning desire to create a freelance lifestyle, so I considered this a learning phase. Meanwhile, I got another extreme experience that shaped my life.

Being a crime reporter was one door that quickly opened and closed for me. Dealing with death is a rite of passage for many journalists and it wasn't long before I was tested. At the time, Beckley had grown into a healthcare center for a nine-county region in the thick of Appalachia. We worked with many good people, several of whom were journalists from outside the region.

Early one Saturday morning, the telephone rang. It was an old college friend who worked for an international news service in the state capital of Charleston, about an hour's drive on a winding mountain road.

"There has been an awful murder in Beckley," Thom told me. "It appears that a teenage boy has killed his entire family." Without hardly taking a breath, he asked if I would go out and report on the incident for the news service, as a freelancer.

I told Ray of the situation, then quickly dressed and drove into the neighborhood where the incident had occurred. I talked to the mother of another teen who lived nearby. She shared that her son had been picked up by the teen in question, in the family vehicle the evening before. As they had driven around town, the teen had shared his horrific story of killing his parents and his two brothers.

Later, I went to the newspaper office, wrote the story and talked to my friend at the news service in Charleston, before returning home. The news of that day became a national story about a family's life that went completely wrong. I thought about Ray and Justin at home. Our home had such life amid this horror.

To say it was a challenge to resume normal life at that point in the evening would be an understatement. I didn't realize at the time, but my reporting skills had been tested to the most extreme limit they would ever get tested in my life.

This horrible situation would affect my vision and, later, determine how my career as a journalist would evolve. I was a sensitive and social person who was naturally inquisitive and loved learning new things. Reporting on this event affected my psyche in a way that I knew was not good. It colored my world a shade that I could not understand, and it revealed to me a dark side of life in which I was unwilling to dwell.

Many of the journalists I know are kind and sensitive people. Many seem to have a sixth sense, or a hunch, when things are not right, when sources are lying, when they know the true facts are being hidden from them.

I can only imagine the affect their work has had on those who have covered crime, investigated murders and the like for decades. As they doggedly seek the truth, their experiences taint their own worlds. It shapes their lives and exposes their inner weaknesses. Several research reports since the year 2001, in fact, have found that journalists suffer from Post-Traumatic Stress Disorder (PTSD) at a rate of 4 to 59 percent, depending on the beats they cover. Those reporting on crime and war seem to be most affected.

As they gain experience, these journalists seem to develop a hardness about them. They draw keen lines between right and wrong. They'll fight for justice, but they will rarely fight for themselves. Journalism, in fact, is a selfless career that requires a person to put all else above themselves. Our college professors told us that we were never part of the story. I disagree. The storyteller is always part of the story.

I never aspired to be a crime (or war) reporter who went home at night to lead a normal life as a parent and partner. Although I admire the people who dedicate their lives to such reporting, that would be rather impossible for me.

By the following year I became the newspaper's lifestyle editor. It was a position that felt right for me, writing about food and homes and families and such.

Shortcut to Success:

Everyone has experiences early in their careers that help them understand what motivates and inspires them. You'll also have experiences that you know inherently aren't a good fit for your personality. Spend some time thinking about your strengths and passions, then move toward a career and a specialty area that feels right.

5. Take the Leap

Crafting a freelance lifestyle may involve a few years of thought and careful planning. If you want to do gig work, take at least three to six months to develop a timeline for your transition.

First, there are some basic logistics. You'll need to create a simple website so that prospective clients can learn about your background, view your portfolio and look at your past successes. Be sure to update your LinkedIn profile and keep your resume current. Every time you pitch a prospective client, they'll look for you online to see if you're qualified for the gig.

I left my full-time editor's position for good after we moved to Savannah, Georgia, where Ray accepted a position as a writer with the daily newspaper. The newspaper editors there also had my resume and samples of my work. We knew from our experience in Beckley that they would likely understand our plight. We were two journalists looking for work, but at least one of us needed a job that involved flexible hours due to parenting demands.

The editors in Savannah also knew that Ray's salary, alone, would not support a family of three. Therefore, they helped me find a lucrative freelance gig.

My flexible work was developing content for special sections being sold by the newspaper's advertising department. The work was somewhat interesting, and the pay was good and on schedule. The ad director was a single guy, a rather young boss who understood the importance of my flexibility and, when he had the chance, even doted on Justin, who showed up for an occasional meeting with me when he was not in preschool. Within a few weeks after completing each special section, like clockwork, I received a check.

This was an arrangement in which I thrived. The more I worked, the more I was paid. On the contrary, if I wasn't working, I was not paid a dime. There were no benefits and no vacation days. But I was eager to spend more time with Justin and ambitious in my work as a writer and editor. This gig felt right.

By now you probably know whether you have the basic skills necessary to launch a freelance business. If you're a writer, you may have also determined your writing niches or specialty areas. If you're a photographer, you probably have an idea about the clients you can serve. If you're a designer, you may already know people who can use your help.

In my own case, my resume told my first client that I was well equipped to do the work they needed done. That client was the newspaper advertising department in Savannah.

Wise Words: How I Made the Leap

By Christopher Johnston

I was 27 and running the business development communications department for the largest architectural / engineering / interiors firm in Cleveland and the entire state of Ohio. A larger firm acquired the company, and my position became redundant. That's when I decided to start freelancing.

The first step: launching my business. I sent my qualifications package to creative directors at advertising and public relations firms throughout northeastern Ohio and then followed up with telephone calls. Some immediately hired me to write a variety of projects. I continued to receive calls for several years from firms that had kept my file.

The second step: sustaining my business. I started pitching editors at every publication I could find that employed freelance journalists. That led to work while building my clip archive in a diverse range of subjects so that I would remain versatile and marketable. I learned quickly to provide value-added services to editors, such as taking photographs or providing a list of potential images. I always asked if they could recommend other editors.

The third step: building a strong business. Other self-employed colleagues encouraged me to connect to a great accountant. He helped me set up my business and financial tools, including hiring an insurance agent and a financial advisor.

The fourth step: expanding my network. I joined supportive organizations such as the Press Club of Cleveland, the Society of Professional Journalists and the American Society of Journalists and Authors. The latter led me to meet my literary agent, who helped me land my first book contract.

The fifth step: Do the work. Every. Day.

Christopher Johnston has published more than 3,500 articles in publications including American Theatre, Christian Science Monitor, History Magazine, Leaps, Johns Hopkins Magazine *and* Scientific American. *His book,* **Shattering Silences: Strategies to Prevent Sexual Assault, Heal Survivors, and Bring Assailants to Justice** (Skyhorse) *was published in 2018.*

It wasn't long before I found another gig. In addition to freelancing at the Savannah paper, I took over the low-paying role of being the editor of the monthly *Tybee News*, on an island near Savannah where we decided to live. Perhaps I had been naïve up until this point, but Georgia is where I was first confronted with outright, blatant racism.

I was visiting a local widow, one of the much older advisory board members for this publication, who proudly flew the Confederate flag on her front lawn, which overlooked the backwaters of Tybee Island.

"I want people to understand which side of the fence I'm on," she said, rather explicitly while several other advisory committee members and I ate a lunch of warm chicken salad and fruit that she served on her screened porch that day.

As a Midwesterner with roots in a region that seems to easily integrate people from all cultures, I was appalled. Perhaps the racism that existed in the Midwest just wasn't as apparent. But this woman's blunt statement provided clarity. I counted it as one important lesson of many in that year that we lived in Georgia.

Soon after, Ray was offered a position back in Columbus and with Justin nearing kindergarten age, we moved north, closer to our families and our own cultural mindsets. That's when my freelance writing career started in earnest as I took assignments from various major newspapers, magazines and other clients around the country.

Shortcut to Success:

Before you take the leap to freelance, do some important tasks. First, create a basic website so that prospective clients can learn about your background and look at your past successes. Be sure to update your LinkedIn profile and keep your resume current. Every time you pitch a prospective client, they'll look for you online to see if you're qualified for the gig. Finally, choose clients that are a good cultural match for you.

Part II

Your Freelance Mindset

1. Find Clients

New freelancers always want to know how to build business. Throughout my career, I have learned three important tips. I call this the lesson of the PPR: people, problem solving and building good relationships.

The first tip I'll share is about people. Business will come fast from people you already know. That doesn't mean that you'll accept all of these business possibilities, but please know that this is where most business opportunities dwell. Here's an example of how this usually works. You may write an article for one editor in a magazine group. When you do a good job, word-of-mouth is a powerful tool. Another editor may then get in touch. I've known many writers who, within a year of working with one editor, realize they have been overwhelmed with assignments from editors within the same organization.

No matter who your first client is, there's a pretty big chance that they will recommend you for other jobs, too.

Now for the issue of problem solving. Generally, there are the clients who will take up a lot of time and won't contribute much to your bottom line.

Have you ever heard of the Pareto Principle? Named after the Italian economist Vilfredo Pareto, this principle establishes an 80-20 rule that says 80 percent of consequences will come from 20 percent of causes. Sales experts will tell you that 80 percent of your business will come from 20 percent of your clients.

If you apply the Pareto Principle to problem clients, some people like to say that 80 percent of your time will be taken up by 20 percent of your clients. That means, as your business grows, you'll probably need to prune out some of those time-consuming clients that aren't major contributors to your bottom line. This act of pruning out clients will allow you to gain perspective and focus for your best clients.

The third tip is about establishing good relationships. You will always need to nurture business relationships. There's no magic to this: Any kind of business takes time and presence of mind. You start by identifying the people who need your services and figure out a way to connect with them so they understand that you can provide help. The more authentic you can be in forming these relationships, the better. Keep clients that pay well, and that respect your time and your abilities.

In finding clients, it is essential to define your target audience. The term target audience is well known among the world's top marketers. Whether it's brand strategy for Target, CVS, Starbucks or another well-known company, the people who are targeted as customers are those who the company attempts to form an emotional bond with so that they keep buying what's offered to them.

After you determine the target audience for your freelance work, there are a few more things that you want to consider. As I've frequently told roomfuls of writers at conferences, you need to figure out what makes you different from every one of your competitors. In other words, what makes you stand out from the crowd of other writers, photographers or designers? As you consider taking the leap to gig work, think about how you can authentically tell your own story in a way that your future clients will connect with you.

In the writing world, freelancers can go two directions. One direction is querying magazine, newspaper and important online editors who may give you freelance assignments. Here's a warning, though. It's a rare writer who's able to earn a living writing only for publications due to the rather low freelance fees paid by so many of them. Those fees can range anywhere from 10 cents a word for local publications to $2 a word by some of the most exclusive national publications. (Producing national articles that pay $2 a word will involve some of the most time-consuming investigative and research work. Those assignments generally go to experienced freelancers who already are working with the publication's editors.)

The second way to build a business is to write content for small and large companies, governmental agencies and nonprofits. If your goal is having a freelance business with a consistent income, you might want to consider going both directions, avoiding any conflicts of interest. That's what I did and so do many other prolific writers. While I wrote for many journalistic publishers, I frequently also took on local clients who needed good, curated content for websites, brochures and such.

With this strategy in mind, many writers have created freelance businesses that match the income provided by their previous full-time jobs. Early in my career, I would add up the fees for childcare, parking and other assistance I'd need if I took a full-time job, which was occasionally offered to me. Every time I added up these expenses, I realized working fulltime and paying for full-time preschool had few financial benefits. By this point, our daughter, Ana, had been born. I was already doing fulfilling work. If I took a full-time job, I wouldn't earn any more money due to the expenses we'd incur.

Wise Words: The Power of Intention
By JoBeth McDaniel

"If you could do anything..."

"I'd freelance for magazines," I blurted, the words tumbling out before Rick, my therapist, finished his question. It happened before I had time to mull over why it made no sense.

At age 24, I saw Rick weekly. I felt adrift after losing my mom to a heart attack, then my fiancé in a fiery breakup. And I hated my low-paying, dead-end office job.

Rick walked me through baby steps to make my impossible dream come true: take a free-lancing class, send out query letters to prospective clients, join a local writers group. Within months, I'd sold a dozen magazine stories written during lunch breaks and at night, earning more money than I thought possible. It felt like magic.

"The power of intention," Rick replied. "You've told the universe what you want. The universe is saying yes." I laughed, amused by his New Age nonsense.

Rick urged me to talk with my dad, a small business owner, about freelancing full time. But my dad was a wreck, too, still lost in his grief. When I finally divulged my secret side career, his mood lifted. "Meet with a bank loan officer," he advised. "Buy a computer. Line up regular clients before saying goodbye to your godawful boss."

"If I fail, will you send me care packages?" I asked, queasy at the thought of leaving my weekly paycheck.

"You know I would," he said. "But I know you won't fail."

His confidence and advice helped me double my income that year. Decades later, I'm still enjoying being my own boss—and appreciating how the power of intention and hard work can combine to create life-changing magic.

JoBeth McDaniel is an author and longtime magazine journalist whose bestselling biography **A Special Kind of Hero** *was named a Library Journal "Best Book" and a Literary Guild selection. Her essays appear in several anthologies, including two college textbooks.*

Freelance work can pay quite well, but it takes a lot of focus to design a career with high financial goals. One of my long-time journalism colleagues, Mabel, was astonished with what she was paid when she began writing marketing copy for a large children's hospital after her journalistic job was cut.

Keep in mind, though, that anyone you know, or you meet, may become your next client. In Mabel's case, as a journalist she was already acquainted with the marketing manager at the children's hospital, so it was easy to approach this person when she began freelancing.

Freelance work can be found even during quick conversations with casual acquaintances. For me, an attorney named Jim became one of those clients. We met through community events and have had an ongoing business relationship for more than 25 years. Early on, I helped Jim develop brochures and mailers for a political campaign and his law office. Later, we worked on strategic content plans for several of his businesses.

Frequently, I am asked by prospective clients—attorneys, doctors, real estate agents, small business owners and publishers—to help them with a writing or editing project. Instead of instantly agreeing, I invite that person to schedule a meeting to discuss their needs.

Ask people their communication challenges and then brainstorm solutions with them, I frequently explain to those wanting to launch a strong freelance business. Then, return to your desk and create a business proposal from what you've learned.

Include a timeline for the project, as well as an estimated cost. Be grateful for the business but, whatever you do, stay professional in the relationship. That means this: Don't give people a cost break just because you like them or they're a friend. No matter how well you know a potential client, the project may bring unforeseen challenges.

It's much better for a project to come in under cost than it is to go over the estimate you've provided.

Shortcut to Success:

Remember the lesson of the PPR: people, problem solving and building good relationships. Your first freelance clients will likely be people you already know. After you create your list of possible clients, schedule meetings and informal conversations with your top five targets.

Meet with each prospective client, email a formal proposal to them, as well as a timeline regarding the work involved. This signals to your client that you are serious about your freelance business. As your business grows, prune out problem clients so that you can better focus on building relationships with those whom you enjoy.

2. Expect to be Paid

If you've never been in business for yourself, the thought that people don't pay their bills may surprise you. But it's true. An important lesson to learn when you're doing gig work is to respect your clients, but just as important is to respect yourself.

Respect yourself enough to earn a decent wage for your work. You can do that with some careful financial planning. One of the quandaries of gig life is sporadic pay checks. When you're considering a freelance career, figure out how much you need to cover household and personal expenses each month.

Why is it important to talk about finances? If we don't, you'll be like me and so many other freelancers were early in our careers. For a few years I didn't establish a business bank account and I didn't pay nearly enough attention to the flow of my freelance revenue. There were some years that I was so busy, in fact, that I didn't realize how much I was earning. (When you earn more than you think you're earning, that means you'll pay a bigger tax bill at the end of the year, by the way.)

Even though it may not be fun to read, this is an important chapter to ponder. No one should start freelancing without giving some careful consideration to the financial aspects of owning a business. To start, open a bank account dedicated to your business and pay attention to the flow of revenue that goes in and out of that account.

If you plan to make freelancing your full-time job, money you earn should cover your monthly expenses, taxes, healthcare insurance and retirement savings. (Taxes, insurance and retirement savings can easily eat up 30 percent of your income so aim high when you're thinking about your financial goals.) Becoming a full-time freelancer is, indeed, a balancing act in so many ways. Therefore, it's important that you get paid well for the gigs that you do.

Eventually you'll have money piling up in that bank account. Once you determine how much you need to cover your personal and household expenses, move that money from your gig account to your personal bank account on a regular basis. For me, it works best to pay myself the first Friday of every month. Then, pay taxes, insurance and retirement savings from your business account. Any business expenses, such as office furniture and technology, should also come out of your business account. If you have money left over after all of that, then you're on your way to doing well in this business!

Now, let's talk about your annual financial goals. If you're a freelancer looking to earn a big income, it's best to have an annual financial goal that challenges you more and more each year. There are a variety of ways that you can achieve that goal, but first let's talk about your current situation.

Are you already freelancing, and looking for ways to improve your income? If so, then keep reading because there are plenty of tips and advice yet to come.

But if you're looking to transition from full-time employment to a freelance career, sometimes the best way to do that is to resign from your full-time position and convince your employer that you can take some of that work with you as a freelancer. Your former employer may become your first anchor client. (An anchor client is one who gives you work on a continuous basis.)

I often coach new freelancers on the steps to transition in this way, generally advising them to plan their resignation at least three months before they speak with their boss so that they have plenty of time to think about their freelance business.

Another way to tackle the issue of transition is to ask your employer if you can go part-time, giving you the freedom and flexibility to pursue other freelance gigs on the side. Several giggers that I know have launched their businesses this way. Early in my career, in fact, I took part-time jobs to stabilize my monthly income. Those part-time jobs were usually within the journalism field, ranging from editing a trade publication to covering the weekly news for a community paper.

✿

At any one time, it's important to know where your revenue will come from over the next three to six months. Set up a simple Excel sheet or another chart of some sort so that you can visualize your expected income over the next several months.

As you're thinking about this, consider three types of clients: anchor clients that regularly give you work, occasional clients that offer projects that sometimes extend over many months, and sporadic clients—such as magazine editors—that may assign you an article once in a while.

Once you examine your month-by-month income, you'll be better suited to set a financial goal for the entire year. Only you can decide on your annual financial goals because every one's fiscal situation is different.

Finally, remember this. Collect the money that is due to you. Don't overlook an unpaid project and don't get emotional about an overdue invoice. Treat these issues as business matters. If an invoice goes unpaid for more than 30 days, follow-up with your client or your client's accounts payable department. Don't accept more business from the client until their account is paid in full.

"Separate money from ego," I explain to new freelancers at conferences where I speak. "Not being paid does not mean you are a bad writer. Don't intermingle your paycheck with your emotions."

Simply ask your client if the check has been cut. If it has not, then ask when you can expect it. Follow up again if you need to. If you must follow up three times, be aware that payment may not come at all. If you are not paid by a client, you have two choices.

Cut your losses and move on, promising yourself that you won't work with that client again. If you choose to do this, retain your dignity and focus on better clients. Your second option is to take that client to small claims court—which will likely result in time (and money) spent and still no payment. It just doesn't really make sense. I learned this lesson the hard way.

One of the biggest mistakes I made in those early years as a freelancer was thinking that my role as a writer was to work *for* other people. After all, when you are a freelancer, you can be at the constant whim of your clients. The mindset goes like this: If you do the assignment as they wish, then a check will fall into your hands. But that doesn't always happen.

Over the years, I've learned that using the word "partner" with a potential client gives a much clearer meaning to your relationship with them. Instead of *working for them*, you are *partnering with them* to solve a challenge that they have. When I email them the initial proposal, I always stress that I look forward to partnering with them.

If you have several clients, you may need to follow up about payment with some of them on a regular basis. One of my hard lessons about this involved a client whom I'll call William. William was an intelligent man who had grown up impoverished.

Sadly, he started robbing banks when he was a teenager and landed in federal prison for 20 years. After he was released from prison, he soared in national prominence as a person who had overcome his obstacles in life and landed a huge contract from a major book publisher.

But William didn't have the temperament or skills to be an author. Thus, he hired several ghost writers before his book was finished. I was among the mix of writers he hired. None of us was ever paid for all our work. I counted those writing hours as a service to humanity.

But I also learned an important lesson here. Never take on a client without signing a payment schedule that you both agree upon.

Shortcut to Success:

Treat freelancing as a business and be cautious as you take on clients. A written agreement that you issue prior to starting the gig will help your client take you seriously as a writer and a business partner. Do not take on any project unless you are sure the person has the money to pay you. Finally, create an annual plan so that you have a roadmap to financial success.

3. Build Bridges

You will work with many good people and many good clients. I met more writers and editors around the country once I began attending conferences in cities throughout the United States. The more professionals I met, the busier I got with assignments from various publications. Meeting other freelancers and working with additional clients helped me build myriad bridges to a variety of career opportunities.

As a freelance journalist by this time, I was working with editors all over the country. It was not unusual for a journalist-friend in another state to contact me with a hot tip about a publication looking for a freelancer.

For the *Chicago Tribune*, I interviewed and wrote about Jody Williams, who won the Nobel Peace Prize for her work clearing the world of landmines. I wrote about the Underground Railroad, toxic shock syndrome, a Croatian dance troupe and much more.

For the *Cleveland Plain Dealer*, I regularly contributed features. One article was about Amish children who were being hidden from their father, who had recently left the Amish sect. I was with their father the day they were found on an Amish farm—crews from ABC's 20/20 news program joined us after reading my initial report. We sadly witnessed strap marks on the children's backs that day. They had been beaten by the family where they stayed. (To this day, that story makes me ill when I think about it.)

Another *Plain Dealer* story was fascinating. I wrote about two professors and their "What If" theories in politics. Often, I've revisited the "What If" theory on my personal level: "What if I'd taken a full-time job and stayed in the world of journalism as an employee?"

For the *Philadelphia Inquirer*, I wrote a travel story about Amish countries in Ohio and Indiana. For a few publications in California, I wrote about health challenges. I did weekly columns for the *Dayton Daily News* and took on assignments from trade publications. I was also assigned stories by various college alumni magazine editors, which have some of the smartest readers you'll ever get.

Occasionally, I wrote an essay that was accepted for publication. Personal essays always need to be written before an editor will commit to buying them. In general, they don't pay a lot, but they can be quite gratifying once they're published.

Based on my writing about a young woman who developed a rare type of cancer after attending high school on a toxic site, I won a grant from the Society for Environmental Journalists and traveled to a New Orleans conference, which resulted in more assignments about the environment.

Wise Words: The Art of Writing a Personal Essay

By Estelle Erasmus

Writing a personal essay works best when you can write about a topic that you are passionate (or obsessed) about. It is a great venue for testing the public's appetite for memoirs in progress, and though it may not pay the bills, it's a byway to landing prestigious bylines and awards.

My students have written about losing a sibling from opioid addiction, the trauma of adoption, and teaching their kids about consent. I wrote about a devastating ectopic pregnancy, becoming a mentor to millennials, and predicting that my future husband would be from another country.

Here are some key aspects of first-person writing.

Create a Flow
A good personal essay has a narrative arc: a beginning, a middle, and an end, and it offers a deeper truth. It can be helpful to focus in on

one person, relationship, memory, moment, event, or object as if you are writing a scene for a movie.

It's All in the Sensory Details

Writing about sight, sounds, touch or taste and what it evoked in you paints a vivid picture and invites the reader into the story.

Instead of writing that you ate a muffin, write, "As I devoured the tart blueberry muffin, I recalled the time I caught my ex-lover feeding the spongy confection into the grasping mouth of another woman."

Find Words That Work

The more common the word, the more readers will overlook it—and your writing. I tell my students to go through their drafts and use a thesaurus to substitute more interesting words. For example, "happy" can become "elated" or "jubilant."

Leave the Reader with a Gift

The reader should get a universal takeaway message, showing that some transformation or learning has taken place.

I wrote this ending for *The New York Times* essay on how I connect with my dad who has Alzheimer's by singing to him.

"So as I face the finality of losing my dad, I will hold on to him as long as I can, with music as our guiding force and new language. Song will let us linger in his past until the wave of Alzheimer's overtakes us both."

Estelle Erasmus is an award-winning journalist and writing coach who writes for The New York Times, The Washington Post *and* WIRED, *and is a contributing editor for* Narratively. *She is an adjunct professor at New York University's School of Professional Studies and writes the "All About the Pitch" column for* Writer's Digest. *She is writing a book on pitching and a memoir. Follow her on Twitter and Instagram at @EstelleSErasmus.*

For a variety of reasons, you may lose touch with editors and other clients. If that happens to you, try to stay connected. You never know who will offer you your next big gig. Years may go by, and an old client will pop up and need your help right at the time when you need work.

Frequently during my freelance career, I have benefited from a long-time client who gets back in touch. Somehow, my schedule has always been open to welcome such clients back into the fold.

But I also blew up a few bridges of my own in telephone conversations with editors who didn't realize that my kids weren't going to go to college, unless that check was in the mail. Ana, our spritely little blond girl with a head full of curls, was six years younger than Justin. She was in elementary school by this point and understood that my work was serious stuff in our house.

Freelance writing was not my hobby. And, although my collections conversations with editors and other clients did not occur often, they at times were necessary.

Be aware that other negotiations will also occur.

"Sherry, can you please take a few photos and send them along to me?" asked an editor from the *Cleveland Plain Dealer* who wanted me to write a story for her section.

"What do you pay for that?" I asked, knowing the assignment that she'd made paid only around $200.

"We don't have an additional budget for photos," she said.

"Well, I can't do additional work without being compensated," I responded bluntly.

"OK," she said through tight lips. "Don't worry about the photos."

Later, I learned that particular editor had made a note to her colleagues that I would be difficult to work with. Fortunately, a few other editors there were also personal friends and knew better. They knew that she had asked me to do a photographer's job without being paid for it. I continued to work with the other editors there.

When I wrote articles for newspapers and magazines, I rarely was asked for a proposal, and I was infrequently given a contract. Instead, an editor would call or email with a potential assignment and would explain a rate of pay for freelancers. Because I was building my portfolio as a writer, I never turned down work. (To this day, editors love writers who never say "no.") Be sure you get your agreement in writing, even a casual email will suffice if it addresses your timeline, a rate of pay and copyrights that will be purchased for that rate.

Shortcut to Success:

Successful freelancers create a lucrative mix of anchor clients and others. Taking on gigs for news organizations, businesses and nonprofits will build your business in various ways. As you gain experience, additional work will come your way with teaching gigs, books that need written, apps that are being developed and other such projects.

4. Search for Work-Life Balance

Work-life balance is an important topic that I never want to overlook when I talk about my career. At this point in time, my weekly work schedule was a hectic one and I used an abbreviated version of childcare.

When our children were preschoolers, I hired college students as babysitters for about 12 hours each week so that I could conduct interviews and schedule necessary appointments. Then, I wrote at night while Ray took over bedtime routines with the kids. Some nights, by 2 a.m., I'd drop into bed next to him, exhausted, yet exhilarated, with deadlines met and stories written. At 7 a.m. the next morning, I'd start all over again. Parenting duties started early in the morning, followed by several periods of research and writing.

As the children grew older, most of my interviews and appointments were scheduled while the kids were at school. By 3 p.m., or so, I'd regroup with them, spending an hour or two with Justin and Ana before making dinner. (I'd cook anything I could within an hour.) Ray would arrive home in time to eat with us.

Following dinner on weekdays, I'd often return to my desk at the rear corner of our family room for a few more hours of work, while Ray finished the dishes, involved the children in folding laundry, helped with homework and did bedtime routines. Every hour, or so, my writing was disrupted by little feet coming back to my doorless office—and I treasured the quick hugs and conversations that the kids offered.

Friday evenings were family nights, and during weekends Ray and I balanced the tasks of entertaining children with other duties. At times, I would schedule writing blocks to be sure I met my deadlines the following week.

On the telephone in my makeshift office one evening, I cried with an older woman in Louisiana as she shared her family history. This story for *Preservation* was a heartbreaking tale of big business winning over the rights of individual property owners. In this case, the descendants of formerly enslaved individuals and share-croppers had inherited the land they were about to lose to a big oil company nearby.

My freelance work was thriving. I was passionate about the topics I covered, but I was only earning about $15,000 a year.

Shortcut to Success:

It's easy for freelancers to work nonstop, allowing their assignments to flow into evenings and weekends. Whether you have a family, or not, value your downtime. Schedule blocks of time to leave your screens, play with the kids, be 100 percent present with your partner, meet with friends, exercise or meditate. Your business will benefit when you nourish yourself.

5. Focus on the Greater Good

If you are lucky in your freelance work, you will meet people who will impact your life. Some of their stories will completely change your life, in fact. That's the case with the story I'm going to share below.

This news article is one that took many hours of research and a large amount of reporting time. Complicated topics will require this. However, after you master a subject, there are a variety of publications that will buy stories on that topic. This is a story I originally wrote for the *Cleveland Plain Dealer* and then later sold related stories to the *Chicago Tribune* and other publications.

Kim looked perfectly healthy the evening that we met. A slight limp was the only visible sign that she had been ill. Kim had been diagnosed with leukemia five years earlier and had survived two bone marrow transplants.

"I'm alive by accident," she told me. "I'm really very, very blessed. There are so few of us who survive this kind of leukemia. I think I've got a purpose. And I'm not there yet. It's for the greater good."

By this point in my career, I had been a freelance writer and editor for about 15 years. I drove to Kim's home that dark autumn evening to hear her side of a story that had divided her hometown, a small Ohio city named Marion.

The story about Marion had been reported by local media outlets for several weeks. Kim had grown up in this town that seemed to be haunted by too many cancer cases among its high school graduates. Yet, the local chamber of commerce officials and others argued that the continued media focus on the cancer hotspot would ruin their thriving business district. My conversation with my editor at the *Cleveland Plain Dealer* was brief when she called to see if I would write a magazine-style story on the topic.

"I'd like to find one person who is suffering the consequences of cancer and tell the story from that angle," I explained to the editor. She agreed and I dove into researching the issue, reading everything I could find about the caustic city meetings during which local residents argued over what could be causing the enormous number of cancer cases in this hotspot.

Kim's mother, Roxanne, was vocal in these news reports, so I called her. "I've been watching this story unfold," I explained. "Will you and your daughter sit down with me to talk about her illness? I'd like to tell your personal story and I don't see any other publication doing that."

Roxanne did not hesitate. She set up a meeting. That cold autumn evening, I talked with Kim, a healthy, vibrant young woman with bright blue eyes and strawberry blond hair.

She had an amazing perspective on a story that was still unfolding around the country. Kim's cancer was an example of what was happening to hundreds, maybe thousands, of other people around the United States who lived in cancer hotspots. In my research a few weeks later, I discovered online a long list of former U.S. military sites where toxins had been dumped after World War I and World War II.

The property where Kim had attended high school was one of those sites. It had served as a military depot, then years later the U.S. Department of Education—which inherited the land—dispersed it to the local school district, where Kim's high school was built.

At age 32, Kim had fought a rare form of leukemia that was usually contracted by much older people.

Despite the successful bone marrow transplant, she still suffered. Steroids she took during her healing process forced her body into early menopause. She would never have children. That made me terrifically sad for her because I so valued being a mother. Kim couldn't cry because the steroids caused her tear ducts to fail.

The evening we talked, Kim was frustrated. No agency or investigator would admit that pollutants on the site of Kim's high school had caused her leukemia. We both knew the statistics, though. The rate of leukemia deaths in Kim's hometown had increased 122 percent over the last 30 years.

Kim clearly believed she was supposed to die nearly four years earlier. She recalled waking up at the hospital after her bone marrow transplant hearing the words: "It's for the greater good." That evening Kim felt that her leukemia was in remission for one reason: so that she could save other lives.

Kim's words, "It's for the greater good," struck me like a bolt of lightning. Goosebumps crept up my arms and tears welled in my eyes. For a moment, I clenched my teeth. That was a trick I'd learned that would avoid tears running down my cheeks when I was doing an interview that made me sad. As journalists do, though, I kept asking questions.

Until five years earlier, Kim had been just like any other young woman. She had been an active and healthy teenager, playing softball in high school, graduating and marrying her husband while she worked as an advertising account executive for a local television station.

"I had a ton of aspirations and things I wanted to do," she confided.

"How she ever lived, I don't know," Roxanne said that evening. "It must be by the grace of God."

"I went in [to the hospital] as a young, aggressive, excited girl. Not scared at all," Kim said. "I came out a 50-year-old."

Kim's mom and some other families affected by unusual cancers started a group called Concerned River Valley Families to demand that the grounds of the high school be tested for cancer-causing substances. By the time Concerned River Valley Families began to ask questions, though, the U.S. Army Corp of Engineering had a list of 9,000 potentially toxic sites nationwide that needed cleaned up. Kim's life, in fact, was making an impact. Eventually, her high school was closed.

Whenever Kim's father, Kent, wearied of the battle to draw attention to his family's concerns, he would remember a night at the hospital when his daughter started grabbing at the catheter in her chest. She said she couldn't fight the leukemia anymore. She told him that she was supposed to die.

Kent held his daughter's hands, preventing her from pulling out the tubing. Then he rang for a nurse.

"It's like everything happens for a reason," he said. "Kim is convinced that she was supposed to die. This is what she's supposed to do, to help in this case, to save lives."

"It's for the greater good" were the words Kim heard over and over in her post-surgical haze, she told me.

Since interviewing Kim, those words have reverberated in my mind for my entire life.

Shortcut to Success:

As your business grows, you will have the opportunity to eliminate gigs that pay well but don't feed your passion or work toward the greater good of society. Whether you are a freelancer or a full-time employee, it's easy to get stuck in a job. If you feel stuck, think more about your passions and how you can make a change to better suit your lifestyle and your focus.

Part III

Working Toward a
Bigger Purpose

1. It's Not About Money

At this point in my career, Kim's story resonated with me. The most important thing to remember in your life is that your career isn't about money. Of course, you need to earn an income, but there's more to your work than just earning a paycheck.

What you do for the greater good with your passion, your intellect, your creativity and your talent will lead you to be both financially and spiritually well off. If your work provides a sense of fulfillment beyond a paycheck, that sense of fulfillment will empower you to create—or work—on behalf of the greater good. You'll also inspire other people along the way.

I've thought a lot about Kim's attitude toward money. "I can't afford writers' block," I said many times during that busy period of my life. With a friend, I started a small writers conference at an inn in the town where we lived. There, every year, I would often reiterate the story of how I launched my freelance career while I coached others who were hoping to do the same.

"My choice in life wasn't writing full-time or quitting," I explained. "I figured out the best way possible to rear my two children. I became a freelance writer."

Kim's words that evening of our interview had a profound effect on me. After that interview, I was clear. If we are working only for the joy and personal contentment of ourselves, then we are not doing what we were put on this earth to do.

If I had some outlandish idea about the work I was doing being more important than anything else in my life, then I was disrespecting myself and my family. If I was taking menial assignments from newspaper and magazine editors just to bring in a few more dollars, then they probably were not worth my time and effort.

My own mother often unknowingly tests my philosophy about the importance of money. My mother loves Las Vegas. In fact, she and my father, both in their 80s, still like to visit. It seems, there's nothing more my mother loves than the flashing lights of a slot machine alerting her to a small victory.

"It's not about money," I've told my mother many times since interviewing Kim.

"It's not?" she'll respond, with a little smile on her round face, her bright eyes flashing.

My mother has a way of making you think that she's carefully considering your idea. Yet, I know her well. At this point, she had already dismissed my notion. My mother had been hungry in her life and, as far as she was concerned, I had not.

For my mother, it *is* about money. She was the tiny daughter, age 3, of a coal miner who died, leaving behind a wife and three children under the age of 5. His death left my grandmother destitute. Mom recalls a time or two when my grandmother would go to the coal mine entrance on payday and hold out a tin cup for donations as the miners emerged from their underground work. These were the days before public welfare.

Maybe the jingle of the slot machines reminds Mom of jiggling coins at the bottom of that cup, I don't know. But six months after Mom graduated from high school, she married my father, Ross, a hardworking man whose mechanically gifted father did not see the value of a college education.

My Dad's father, Charlie Beck, was excited about cars. Just north of Ohio, in Michigan, Henry Ford had founded an automotive company in 1899, about eight years before Charlie was born. The idea that cars could be created on an assembly line told Charlie that help would be needed in repairing them. He learned the trade of being an auto mechanic and supported his wife and three children, my father being the oldest, with his earnings. Charlie Beck had figured out how to make a good living without a college degree and, apparently, he expected his children to do the same.

As a young father, Dad started out in sales, selling life insurance among other things. Then, he followed an entrepreneurial path when he started several small businesses and sold a couple of them. Finally, for the last 20 years of his career, regular pay and benefits enticed him to join the Teamsters and drive a steel truck.

When I consider my freelance career and the various passions I've developed throughout it, many are often explained with my family's history. My drive for entrepreneurism, absolutely, came from my father. My dire motivation to succeed, likely from my mother. But I've developed other passions, too. One is about how the context of history influences our lives.

My grandmother and Charlie's wife, Myra Roberts Worthington Beck, was the daughter of Quakers whose ancestors arrived in Philadelphia on one of the three ships that traveled with William Penn from England. The family first settled in Bucks County, Pennsylvania, but eventually drove horses and carriages over the Allegheny Mountains to be among the founders of the first Quaker meeting house west of the mountains in Mount Pleasant, Ohio.

Later, many of the Mount Pleasant Quakers were involved in the Underground Railroad during the mid-

19th century, hiding formerly enslaved people in their homes and barns as they fled the south, traveling north to find freedom.

Although they were not wealthy, Mom and Dad both came from religious families that were rich in high morals and good ethics. My parents had seen the evils caused by alcoholism in their own families, so they didn't drink or smoke. Mom's grandparents came to America from Poland. They practiced Catholicism and settled in eastern Ohio's coal camps. When Mom married Dad, it seemed she had married well. Before she was 24 years old, she had given birth to three of her four daughters.

As I grew up the second oldest of those daughters, I had always been taught the unspoken rule that life on this earth was a gift and we repay that gift by living generously for the greater community. This was not something we discussed in my family, but we learned modeling our lives in the way that our parents and grandparents lived. Work hard, care about others.

"Take care of family first," was Dad's take on life.

It was taboo to talk about yourself and your work, especially if you were successful at it. Certainly, in the Beck family, it was taboo to even talk about the sacrifices one makes in life when it comes to raising a family.

"All of my daughters are smart and beautiful," Mom would say when any one of us was complimented for any achievement. In fact, there were many compliments as my sisters and I excelled in school, two graduated at the top of their classes. Two of us were more socially inclined, both serving as class presidents.

Today, all three of my sisters still excel at their respective career paths—and I am terrifically proud of each of them. One is a doctor of pharmacy using her extensive knowledge to inform healthcare leaders and investors on current pharmaceutical trends. Another has a master's degree in health sciences and has spent her career focused on various respiratory issues, even editing the world's first textbook on neonatal respiratory care. The third, a long-time educator, is focused on the inequities of public education and has also just received her doctorate degree.

Despite living in an era of the 1950s and 1960s in which women rarely worked outside the home, Mom investigated job opportunities. At one point, she decided to become a correspondent for a local newspaper—and that probably affected my career path. Eventually she went to a technical school to become a licensed practical nurse. After a brief period emptying bedpans and passing out medications in a nursing home, she settled in as a social worker for the local juvenile court system.

The fact that she had successfully reared four daughters was among her credentials. The local judge cold-called her with the job offer.

Shortcut to Success:

Consider your family background and how it feeds into your desire to do independent gig work. Oftentimes what we are told as children must be carefully sorted out before we are able to fully understand ourselves and our own motivations. Once we know who we are as individuals, it becomes easier to clear a path for career success.

2. Opportunities Knock

If you believe that you are capable of starting a freelance business or transforming your life in another way, you can make it happen. That transformation, though, may not always be easy. At times, I've had to look in the mirror to convince myself that I'm capable of the challenge that lies ahead.

The motivation to make a big change in your life and your lifestyle must come from deep within yourself. Indeed, deciding to leave full-time employment in favor of gig work is a big decision. However, the flexibility and fortune that can await those who are passionate about freelancing will reaffirm your decision to make the change.

I have reconsidered my freelance path several times. About 12 years after I'd been a full-time freelancer, I decided to take on a full-time job that involved being the editor/publisher of a weekly newspaper. Honestly, with both kids in school I thought the time had come to go back to an office job.

James, a journalism graduate from the University of Missouri who had gone further to get a Harvard MBA, was a group publisher who oversaw several daily newspapers in the region. He was my boss. As part of his job, he was buying this weekly, which would be among the collection he was putting together for a corporate newspaper group.

I was torn when making this decision. My gut was saying, "No, thank you." And I wouldn't be telling the truth if I didn't admit seeing the red flags flying. Yet, I persisted, refusing to yield to the warning signs.

Certainly, this was not a job I had been seeking. James found my name on a short list of potential leaders that the former newspaper owner had provided to him. That owner knew I was a prolific freelance journalist, always working at deadline pace in addition to delivering her news reports as a volunteer for local community organizations.

I was intrigued with the idea of holding this full-time position. By this point, I'd been staying up nights and working weekends, freelancing for more than a dozen years. Honestly, I thought this job would bring more sanity to our family life.

That sunny spring afternoon when James interviewed me, we talked about newspapering a lot. But he also shared that his wife, Julie, did freelance work. He, in fact, suggested that I could continue freelancing while I worked for him. In the end, he offered me the job and I accepted.

Covering the news of a tiny community wasn't the best fit for me in the town where we were rearing our children. The job impacted every moment that I was in public. I could not stop at the local grocery store without Ana or Justin also being immersed into a conversation about politics.

Per James' remark, I was determined to continue my freelance work. I especially remember a miserable assignment that put me in the position of working while the rest of my family took a weekend break to visit with friends. I started the full-time job on Memorial Day and resigned by mid-December. In my gut, I knew a change was required. That position pulled me 100 percent away from my home and family.

Even though I had more than doubled my earnings, I felt as though I would miss the remainder of my children's childhoods in favor of managing a small newspaper staff and hitting a weekly newspaper deadline.

James was gentle when I told him I was resigning to resume my full-time gig work. He quickly started looking for my replacements, hiring both an editor and a publisher in my place. The day I returned to my home office, two extra-large poinsettias and a gracious thank you note were delivered to our home's front door. I was certain I'd never see James again. Still, I was impressed with the grace and dignity in which he handled my resignation after only a short time at the helm.

Shortcut to Success:

Carefully consider each opportunity before you decide to accept or reject it. Following are some questions that you might ask yourself:

- Does this opportunity fit into the career path I've designed?

- Does this opportunity pay me enough for the work I'll be doing?

- If you have a family, ask: "How does this opportunity affect my family life?"

3. Accumulating More Skills

Part of the way that you begin valuing yourself is placing a value on your skill set. After all, that editor or client would not be contacting you if they could do the job themselves, right?

Unless you are being paid a high hourly rate to be on call in the role of a crisis communications advisor or a similar job, then there is no need to always be available to your client. Set your office hours and designate times that you'll respond to texts, emails and phone calls. Never feel like you must be available to a client 24/7 unless that is in your contract, and you are being compensated well to do so.

After leaving the editor/publisher job, I successfully put together the puzzle of fulfilling work and family life. I engaged with several editors who appreciated my work—even if I wasn't onsite. I took on bigger editorial projects. And I began teaching a journalism class at a liberal arts college that grew into a 20-year relationship with that college, some semesters teaching up to three courses.

The editor of the city magazine where Ray worked offered me a regular gig: writing about fabulous homes in the Central Ohio area. Ray's position at the same magazine required that he write about the powerful families who lived in the area.

Columbus Monthly was well-received in the community for its hard-hitting insight into the people who ran the city. As a business model, city and regional magazines are different from newspapers. Subscribers are generally better educated, have higher incomes and more power than others around the region.

Outstanding among those powerful people in Central Ohio was one man, a single guy at the time, who was an emerging leader. Les Wexner was the founder of a retailing giant that included brands such as Victoria's Secret, Bath and Body Works, Abercrombie & Fitch and others. In fact, at this time, even as a Columbus native, he spent more time in New York and traveling the world on behalf of his brands.

Still, Wexner was the talk of the town. A billionaire, he had quietly spent many years using a $5,000 loan from an aunt to launch his business and build his retail empire. As Wexner became more involved in the civic affairs of Columbus, his disruption among the powerful people already running the city was palpable. (Later, Wexner's relationship with the late Jeffrey Epstein would come under intense, international scrutiny.)

Around this same time, Wexner had decided to build his own town. Quietly, his colleagues bought up a lot of property around a small farming community outside of Columbus named New Albany.

His first priority was building a 60,000-square-foot mansion of his own. A few years later, at age 55, he married, and his wife had four children within five years.

Next door to the Wexner compound sprung up a variety of large homes in an area called New Albany Farms. It wasn't long after the first residents moved in that I drove through its gated entrance.

Near the end of the main road that wound past these mansions, Dr. Adolph Lombardi and his wife, Anne, warmly welcomed me into their large, new home. It was a remarkable interview that evening, partly because Dr. Lombardi explained his work. As a young physician, he was a pioneer of joint replacement surgeries. He and two colleagues invented a knee joint prosthesis that was patented in 1999.

Dr. Lombardi and his wife were casual that evening as they showed me around their 8,000-square-foot home, filled with Victorian antiques that their interior designer had discovered. The Lombardi's interior designer, Dennis McAvena, and I became professional colleagues for many years. As a designer, Dennis understood gig work and became one of the most prolific designers used by New Albany residents. He often recommended homeowners to be featured in the magazine because they were generous in enabling him to do his creative work.

The Lombardis were a warm and friendly family, and Adolph shared the stories from his life as though to qualify the reasons why he had built a fabulous home for his own family, which by then involved young children. Dr. Lombardi had grown up in a family of limited means in a Philadelphia rowhouse.

Science may have been his area of expertise, but it was apparent that Dr. Lombardi had a passion for design. His interior designer told me about getting a call upon the doctor's return from Italy one day. Dr. Lombardi had purchased a church pew from an antique dealer and had it shipped, in its rough condition, to his New Albany home. It would become Dennis's job to have 200 years, or more, of grit removed from it, have it reupholstered and help position it in the Lombardi's massive family room.

Dr. Lombardi very clearly was working toward a greater good. He was the first of many more entrepreneurial inventors I've known.

Shortcut to Success:

You will know in your gut when your career path is on track. As you begin valuing yourself and the time you invest in your career, you likely will take note of others who are making major contributions toward the greater good. Your ability to connect and tell the stories of people who have accomplished things much bigger than your own will enrich your career and motivate you for years to come.

4. The Importance of Being Present

We've talked a lot about respecting yourself enough to be sure that you're working with clients that are the right cultural match for you, and to be certain that you'll be paid for your work. Now, let's talk about having respect for your clients.

Wise Words: Stay Connected
By Michelle V. Rafter

One of my first freelance assignments was for the trade magazine I'd just quit to travel in Europe. I convinced the publication's owners to pay me to cover a conference and press junket from overseas. When I returned six months later, the magazine remained a go-to client.

That was 30-plus years ago. Since then, my writing career has gone through multiple iterations. Through it all, I've relied on staying close to past editors and clients for a good chunk of my work. It's easier to get a "Yes" from someone who knows and values my abilities than to cold pitch—plus, who needs the rejection?

I've collaborated with more than a dozen editors as they've moved from one publication to another. Sometimes years, or decades, pass between gigs. A business book I ghostwrote in early 2021 was a project I got from the owner of a content agency who I first worked with at that trade magazine. An editor at a Catholic press who I know from our college newspaper days tapped me to write a book proposal.

There's no big secret to staying connected. Bring your "A" game to every assignment, so as editors move, they're happy to bring you along. Be meticulous, but easy to work with. Stay in touch, even when you're not looking for work. Follow people online. Meet for coffee. Connect at industry events. If you worked with an editor that year, send them a thank you in December to show your appreciation.

Working with previous clients has given me more than work. It's given me lasting friendships that have enriched my freelance career.

Michelle V. Rafter is a Portland, Oregon, ghostwriter, reporter and editor. Her work has appeared in national business, trade and consumer publications.

One way you respect your clients is to be completely present when you are talking to them. Understand their needs and their challenges. Look into their eyes when you talk to them. Ask questions to clarify your understanding of their business so that you can do the gig they've offered in the best possible way.

On one of the assignments to write about a wonderful home, I drove into the gated Edge of Woods neighborhood, just a half mile away from the New Albany Country Club. There, at the end of the court, I was greeted by Jeanne McCoy and her designer, who gave me a grand tour of what was a new home. The house was built for Jeanne and her husband, John G. McCoy, for their retirement.

John G. McCoy was an entrepreneur. He was the founder of Bank One, which eventually was integrated with JPMorgan Chase & Co. He was an inventor of what we now know as the credit card industry, building a strong card business that helped Bank One become what the *New York Times* estimated as an $8 billion business. Eventually, the bank was worth even more as it later merged with JP Morgan.

When I started out in my freelance career, the credit card services division of what was then called Banc One was one of my first clients. It was because I had done that gig that I understood the innovation John G. McCoy had created: Banc One contracted with retailers to issue credit cards under the retailer's logo.

The credit card icon John G. McCoy made a cameo appearance that day I visited his home, just before he left for the office he still visited daily. Their son, John B. McCoy, was running Bank One at the time.

One of the many things that Jeanne shared during that visit was her wrapping room—a space on the second floor where she kept well organized rolls of colorful wrapping paper, ribbons, tissues to stuff boxes and gift bags and plenty of Scotch tape. Jeanne's wrapping room never made it into the magazine spread, yet it is still a clear visual in my mind. It's almost as if her generosity was emphasized by the mere existence of that room.

Not a holiday or a birthday passes when I'm wrapping a gift that I don't think about Jeanne and the many wonderful thoughts she shared with me that day. Even though she had moved from a much larger home, Jeanne instructed that keeping those things nearest and dearest to one's heart was what was important in downsizing a home.

Her kitchen backsplash featured hand-painted tiles depicting scenes from the family's Michigan gathering place. There was nothing really special in the scenes, except the fact that I knew she deeply treasured the presence of her own children and grandchildren.

Jeanne McCoy was generous in her thoughts and humble during the time we spent together that day. This interview taught me important life lessons: Appreciate the people around you and a few precious things. Nothing else really matters that much.

In the following years, I interviewed many more homeowners who were similar to the McCoys. Friendly and kind, they were generally quiet about the things that they are able purchase, instead talking more frequently of their humble beginnings and their families.

Often, in fact, they refused to be named in the magazine, and I have always had a policy of granting that wish. Homeowners have frequently told me in interviews that their lives have been very blessed. The McCoy family and some others are the quiet philanthropists of our time. I've learned much about a person's generosity of spirit when I have visited their home.

Shortcut to Success:

Career success comes to writers and others who are present in casual conversations, interviews and formal meetings. Always show up on time, participate to your fullest capabilities and be responsive to what people say. This is a key to freelancers and anyone else who is building a business. You never know where your next opportunity will be—or who will give you a lot of work throughout your career.

Part IV:

Inspiration and Passion

1. Profit Flows from Passion

My creative energy was ignited when I wrote about grand homes such as those owned by the Lombardis and the McCoys. The architectural elegance of each home, coupled with the creative work of the interior designers, architects and builders who were involved, sparked my enthusiasm for telling these stories.

I had to carefully consider my business plan, though. The money I earned writing about homes for a regional magazine did not at all match the buzz that was created each time an article was published. When you know the work you are doing is more valuable than what you are being paid, it's time to reassess your strategy. For me, that time had come.

I decided to take on a major gig that was somewhat outside the bailiwick of my freelance writing work. The National Inventors Hall of Fame Foundation contracted with me to market and promote their summertime science camps for children.

Ray and I had become a couple that celebrated creativity any time the chance arose. The creative process, when put to work as a writer, designer, artist or scientist, can change the world. The creative energy that drove my writing would now also drive my appreciation for those who launched big inventions.

By this time, Ray and I each had spent hours of volunteer time coaching a total of 19 Odyssey of the Mind (later called Destination Imagination) teams in which Justin and Ana had participated. I so valued the program that focused on creative problem solving that I volunteered to lead the local charge for the school district and helped many other parents establish teams for their own kids.

This new gig promoting Camp Invention with the National Inventors Hall of Fame Foundation created no conflict of interest with my other freelance work, so I quickly signed the contract. As a journalist, writing promotional copy, communicating with educators, news media and such was easy. In fact, I had done just that as a board member and volunteer communications chair for many local organizations.

Eventually, I was offered a full-time position with NIHFF to set up a national communications office for the camp programs. During that time, I frequently emailed and spoke with producers of major talk shows—Jay Leno, Ellen DeGeneres, Oprah Winfrey, Martha Stewart and others.

"What have the children invented?" those producers would often ask in follow-up calls, as they decided whether to invite children on their shows. I often thought about Dr. Lombardi and other inventors whom I personally knew.

"As is the case with any inventor, this one-week camp is not nearly enough time for a child in elementary school to actually create an invention," I'd respond. "What this program provides, though, is the basis for creative thinking. We encourage children to take risks, learn to fail and have a lot of fun as they create and test new ideas."

I still love it when people put thoughts into action by creating something—a painting, a product, a business or anything. Even though working with Camp Invention made summertime extremely busy, it stroked my desire to be a spokesperson on behalf of creativity.

My work with the National Inventors Hall of Fame also introduced me to many more inventors, as I attended annual induction ceremonies. At one luncheon, I sat across from the chemist Lloyd Conover, the inventor of tetracycline, an antibiotic that Justin and Ana had been prescribed through the years. It was a surreal moment to chat with Conover, a scientist who had created such a legacy and had earned more than 300 patents as an inventor.

The stories of the men and women who have worked hard on patents, invented earth-shattering breakthroughs and reaped millions of dollars from their production astonished me. My spirit was continually lifted by these creative geniuses. I was in awe of their passion for discovery and far more impressed by their processes than I was by their abilities to earn a lot of money from their patents.

Meanwhile, I balanced those intensive summers filled with Camp Invention with academic teaching and the writing of dozens of freelance articles. We had slowly updated our 1920s home. My office space had a wonderful window that looked out over our sloping backyard and the bike path that settled into the valley below it. During my daydreaming as I would write each day, I envisioned French doors that would open and a broad back porch where I could soak in a few minutes of the morning sun.

Likely, my vision was influenced by the designers, architects and builders that I interviewed. So, I convinced Ray that he was capable of building a monolithic deck. The suggestion caused nightmares of the deck crashing, but he persevered, and the project was soon accomplished.

At this point in my life, my passion for creativity fueled my motivation for work. Even though I spent a lot of time balancing my various projects, I was gratified with my accomplishments. Rarely was I bored, and I was earning more than I had ever expected.

Shortcut to Success:

Volunteer work can turn into a lucrative gig. After spending many years as a volunteer in various organizations, my strength as a communicator went to work for a cause I was passionate about. In this case, that cause was educating and encouraging the next generation of potential inventors. The most successful freelancers I know balance their work with projects of passion. It helps when those passion projects also pay well.

2. Making a Grand Pivot

Learning to pivot is essential for your work life and even more important if you are a gigger. Once the Camp Invention season ended each August, I actively looked for ways that I could pursue my writing passions.

I applied and received a small grant from the Fund for Investigative Journalism. By now, it had been about three years since meeting Kim in Marion. There were hordes of toxic waste sites around the country. I had collected a box of research about the Defense Environmental Restoration Program, which looked after these former military sites and the suspected toxins within them.

I queried an editor at *The Washington Post* Sunday Magazine. My research had shown that the Post had published little on the topic addressing regions outside of Washington, D.C., which had several toxic sites of its own on the list.

Wise Words: Follow Your Passion
By Andrea King Collier

I have been at this writing game over 30 years. I love being able to mix it up and follow my passions. I love cooking, so I write about food. I love books, so I do book reviews. I get to sit down and write essays about things that matter to me. I even write books when I have a burning idea. I get to talk to people who are doing amazing things.

My latest passion is something I couldn't have seen coming—visual storytelling. When I was in journalism school at Indiana University, I got a D in photography and vowed that I would never take another picture. Fast forward to 2010.

I was bored with reporting, wanting to go do something else. I went to two screenings—one was Timothy Greenfield-Sanders' "The Black List," a gorgeously photographed documentary of famous Black Americans telling something about themselves that most people wouldn't know. And the next day I went to the premier of Spike Lee's documentary, "If God is Willing and Da Creek Don't Rise" about post-Katrina New Orleans. I wept for two days.

Those two works and things like the Humans of New York gave me permission to explore storytelling without being boxed in. I see everything as story now. It even led to me taking to the Mainstage at the Moth Story Hour to do old school oral storytelling.

I love my work. I turn 65 this year and I can't imagine what retirement would look like.

Andrea King Collier is a Michigan-based award-winning multimedia journalist and author. She is also a Moth storyteller.

❧

A week or two later, I sat at my computer with tears rolling down my cheeks as I watched the television coverage of 9/11. I had returned from teaching two morning college classes, each of which were direly affected by the events unfolding in New York City and at the Pentagon. I picked up Ana at school that afternoon, and we returned home to watch more of the coverage.

The events that day disrupted my work on that toxic project. Not just for the day, but for years to come. As a student reporter at the University of Maryland, Justin had already covered the halt of all air traffic and its effects on the country's first airport established by the Wright brothers in College Park. Skies overhead were quiet in those days immediately following the tragic attack that killed so many.

But jets from Wright-Patterson Airforce Base in Dayton awoke me one night, flying over our home on their way to Afghanistan or Iraq. I knew that my work on the DERP sites would be set aside as the United States entered a war that would likely spill more chemical toxins and activate landmines now across the Middle East.

A few months later all my research on the DERP sites was boxed and put into storage. Ray and I sold that house and renovated a 100-year-old house across town. One thing freelancing had taught me was to pay close attention to trends that would stabilize my earnings and predict my success as a writer. Now was not the time to pursue the environmental project. Instead, I moved on to other things, promising myself that I would return to this gig in years to come.

Shortcut to Success:

A local, national or global crisis can change the way a freelancer works. Being able to leave an important project behind and move on to the next one will be crucial to your long-term success in establishing a firm business. If you choose projects that are important to you, then you will always be energized in your work.

3. Becoming a Book Author

I'm a fan of quiet chats with close friends, and there's something important I want you to know. Anytime you schedule lunch, coffee or dinner with a friend or a new acquaintance, you are likely building business in a way that may not be revealed for many years to come. Many times, those conversations have resulted in additional work.

My work as an author started out this way. After 9/11, there seemed to be a greater need for stories that could help children understand what was going on in the world, and my work as a book author grew.

My first book editor, years earlier, was the late Tracy Dils, who was also an author. She and I had met at an early writers' group where about six writers would talk over our projects and consider fresh options. Tracy and I had much in common. We were the exact same age and she had grown up and left the town where I currently lived. In other words, my history in Granville started soon after her history there ended.

One evening, Tracy announced that she had just taken a job as an editor for a new publishing company. Soon, I accepted an assignment: writing a children's microwave cookbook. This was a fun, albeit nauseating project, because at the time I was developing recipes and writing the book, I was also pregnant with Ana. I must admit, not every recipe seemed as mouthwatering as the photos in the paperback book made it look.

My next book-writing adventure involved creating six workbooks called Master Study Skills for a newly formed educational book company. I learned a lot from that exercise of creatively coming up with new activities for children in grades one through six and working through several months of grueling deadlines. For one, I learned that writing educational workbooks was challenging for someone without a degree in education.

But more than that, I also learned during that time that whole companies will be built on the work of creative individuals. They will pay you what seems to be a lot of money to create products that they will use over and over again. In fact, that company was later sold by its original owners. We writers contracted by the first company weren't compensated for anything beyond our original work. Imagine my surprise to see a whole new line of workbooks bearing my name when I was visiting a bookstore one day.

It's imperative as a gigger that you read contracts, offer them to clients and structure any agreement that you make with a client. I learned that there were times I would sign away my copyrights as an author, and that there were other times that I would maintain those rights as my own. The choice was always mine.

If you are working with a publisher, it's always best, as an author, to sign an agreement that provides a book advance followed by royalties based on sales numbers.

Avoid any offer to buy your book for a flat fee or under a work-for-hire contract. Some of the prolific writers I know now self-publish all their books. They shoulder some upfront costs, but they also earn more revenue from each book sale.

My relationship with Tracy is one of those that continued for several years. About a decade after we first met, I casually mentioned that I was writing a freelance article for the *Chicago Tribune* about Nobel Peace Prize winner Jody Williams and her work around the world eliminating landmines. Weeks earlier I had attended a Minnesota conference where I'd interviewed Jody. Tracy mulled over my news as she chewed.

"You should propose her as a topic for a book for Chelsea House," she said. She was already writing a book for middle school students for the Philadelphia-based company, and she knew they were looking for new authors. "I'll give you my editor's email address there."

That one email immediately resulted in two book assignments and, later, many more. "I'm sorry, the committee did not approve Jody Williams as one of our topics this year," the editor said during an apologetic email. "Would you like to write about one of the women from the list below instead?"

I chose two: Katie Couric and Olympic ice-skating star Michelle Kwan, and wrote both books in the following year. My relationship with Chelsea House continued, writing nearly a dozen books in the decade that followed. Often the company gave short deadlines and I signed contracts that said I would complete a book in four to six months. In the beginning, I attempted to arrange interviews with my subjects.

"I'm sorry, Katie will agree to interviews for magazine articles but not for books," I recall Katie Couric's publicist telling me. Katie's first husband had died not long before this, so I completely understood her response.

The more books I wrote, the easier they became. The stories of these successful women propelled me. Writing about Oprah's childhood in Mississippi when her grandparents couldn't afford shoes for her, writing about Ellen DeGeneres' first television show that was cancelled because she came out as a lesbian, writing about Martha Stewart's passion for entertaining and a subsequent jail sentence for insider trading—these were amazing women whose stories needed told to the middle school girls who had hopes and dreams for their own futures.

You develop a passion for work when you realize it will shape the lives of people who read it. I had a sense of purpose in writing these books. Partly, I loved writing these books because it was a challenge to find books about women in pop culture. I watched at the local library as Ana tried to find women she was interested in reading about for assignments she was given in middle school.

Writing these books about strong women who had built big careers was nearly an addictive gig. The youngsters in middle schools around the country could learn valuable lessons from the lives of these awesome people. For years after they were written, I received letters from students who read and enjoyed these stories.

You may wonder how I integrated being an author into my other deadlines and work. Through some trial and error, I created a simple system that made writing these books much easier.

I paid college interns to do intensive research uncovering television transcripts, magazine and newspaper articles, court documents, academic journals and anything else that I could use. The intern working on a specific book would highlight important information in each article and then file it in chronological files, organized by the chapters I had outlined for them.

Once the research was completed and my files organized, I started reading and I learned that many of my subjects had a common trait. Persistence paid off. Many had invested years in their careers before they became household names.

For Katie Couric, who rose to the top of the *Today Show* as one of television's most popular anchors, this was true. As a woman operating in a man's world of network television, her sunny smile never showed the stress of tough contract negotiations to get a salary that might equal her male counterparts.

If you are hungry, like Oprah Winfrey was growing up, you'll work hard to buy the food and clothing you need. Then, later, you'll help the greater good when your earnings are far beyond what you could have ever imagined. If you are smart and creative, like Oprah, you'll figure out a pathway to be even more successful by syndicating your television show and creating your own television network. Oprah's work on behalf of the greater good continues to awe me.

If you don't have a college degree, you may fall back on your singular dream. For Ellen DeGeneres, that dream was becoming a comedian. She overcame many obstacles to meet her current success.

By the time I finished each book, I swore I would never write another.

"I've left book hell for good," I would tell Ray. He would rub my shoulders, we would go for a long walk and, later, open a bottle of red wine.

He knew I would take another book assignment. He knew because he is a kindred spirit in the world of writers. Our hearts beat for good storytelling and without the ability to do that, we both understand that we may not be able to survive.

Still, I strived for work-life balance. Being social and being in the community has always been important to me and a good reason to walk away from the computer.

My time writing has been balanced with community activities—being president of a parent-teacher organization, vice president of the local music boosters, launching an academic booster's group, chairing a community carnival—or even a gala. For our family, these activities and more immersed the four of us into community life. We made good friends and spent hours on soccer fields, at tennis courts and during band competitions talking and connecting with other parents.

By now, I had cobbled together a career that created earnings of more than $100,000 each year. My gig income began soaring over Ray's, while he worked as a full-time editor.

Remember this: Opportunities will come your way because people will see your passion for your work from the very minute they meet you. The more gratified you are with your work, the more it will seem to multiply.

Before I leave this chapter about books, though, there's something else I want to tell you. Many people have asked me for advice about how to become an author. "I still call authoring a book, my weekend work," I tell them. "You can't let go of your other work so often you'll find yourself doubling up. If I help you write a book, it's going to cost you a lot of money."

Being an author, in most cases, just doesn't make financial sense. In fact, a survey released by the Author's Guild in 2019 showed that the average salary of responding authors was less than $7,000 per year. News reports of six-figure advances given to celebrities and politicians skew the reality that most authors know.

In my life, there is nothing more that has resembled the miracle of pregnancy and childbirth than publishing a book. Most authors will tell you that there's a fair amount of anxiety and anguish involved in producing a book of 50,000 or more words.

Months will go on as you attempt to make some sense with your writing. But it's really quite magical as words begin to flow, as you're filling pages with the knowledge that you've gathered. Still, without a good editor, you will be unsure that your story is any good at all.

Until you've written a book, you may not understand what I mean. Putting hands to the keyboard to produce one is an endurance test of both mental and physical preparedness.

When you are writing a book, your body may take a beating. The worst-case scenario, perhaps, will be what the renowned late author Pat Conroy went through. He suffered nervous breakdowns while writing many of his books. For an article I was writing, I interviewed him just after he released a book about his college basketball career, *My Losing Season*. He told me that this was the first book he'd written that did not cause a mental breakdown. (If you're a student of Conroy, you will understand that much of his early writing detailed the abuse he suffered at the hands of his father.)

At minimum, when you write a book, you may sit too long. You may eat too much. Or, too little. Maybe you'll drink too much wine or participate in other mind-altering activities. You'll likely avoid friends, avoid phone calls. Postpone doctors' visits. Delay parties and celebrations. Book writing will go on for months and months. Then your book will finally be finished, and the celebration and preparations for its birth will begin.

When I was teaching and juggling multiple other deadlines, I always loved the open-endedness of a Saturday or Sunday morning free of other deadlines and business obligations as I sat at my laptop and told what I considered to be important stories. I would take my laptop from my messy office and settle quietly in the living room of our big, old home. There, with few things to distract me, I would write until it felt like my brain was wrung dry for the day. With any luck at all, I had met my goal of producing one chapter a day.

With the biographies that I wrote, I knew the young people who read these books in middle school could learn valuable lessons from the lives of these awesome women. Even though my fiscal profit from this writing was low, the deposit I was making into the bank of knowledge for future generations felt right.

During the time I was producing numerous books, I was caught in a dizzying schedule of various types of work, major deadlines and little-to-no time available to regroup and regenerate. Most evenings, Ray and I would unplug from our computers, go to the refurbished attic in the 100-year-old home that we had just finished paying a contractor to renovate, pop open the skylights and relax in the cool autumn air while we caught up on the day's news.

Granville provided the perfect balance between creation and contentment. It's a good thing if the place where you choose to live can do that.

Shortcut to Success:

Gig opportunities will abound when you connect and network among others like you. Work-life balance is a lifetime struggle for many people who build their own businesses. Be sure that you have the time to do all the work that you accept, while still maintaining a balanced lifestyle.

4. Have a Branding Viewpoint

Your biggest hurdle in your career life will be overcoming your own fears and your loftiest leap will be one of faith. But it will be a leap that you take because, after all, you have faith in yourself that you will not fail. Having that faith, though, takes a ton of confidence. Trust after you've spent five or 10 or 20 years in your career, you will have acquired new skills and new talents.

As you acquire skills and accumulate successes, people will ask you to take on new roles or assignments for which you may not feel prepared. Have confidence in yourself that you can get that job done. Listen to your gut. If you trust the person making the request, then there's probably a reason you need to seriously consider the assignment.

There will be many times in your life that you will need to reassess your career choices and you may not even have the time to realize that. For me, it wasn't that I disliked my work. In fact, it was that I liked my work too much. All of it.

During the academic year, I continually responded to dozens of teachers working with Camp Invention and my journalism students at the college. Two days a week I arose each morning around 5:30 a.m. to teach an 8 a.m. class. As other professors trickled into the department, when class ended at 9:50 a.m.—if I wasn't teaching again that day—I rushed back to my home office and picked up some fast food along the way for lunch. Once back at my computer, I dove into the other writing and communications that awaited me there.

The alumni magazine editor for Denison University was one of those who was consistently in touch, always dangling writing assignments before me even though my time to accept them was limited.

One day that editor emailed a note asking if I'd be interested in rebranding another small college's magazine. "It was so bad that the provost there has killed the magazine," he said. "The college president wants a completely new version."

I accepted the challenge and began working on the new Marietta College Alumni Magazine as a contracted editor. Just when I thought I couldn't get any busier, I did.

My annual attendance at the conference of the American Society of Journalists and Authors in New York provided a rare time for me to regenerate with like minds and reassess my goals.

"I'm going to attend the ASJA conference in May," I told Ray one winter day. "I have plenty of work, but what if I talk with some editors and agents about a biography on Les Wexner, as the grandfather of all branding."

Ray still worked full-time as an editor, still regularly interviewing Wexner. We were both working nearly seven days a week.

He and I agreed that if we caught interest from a

publisher regarding the Wexner book, I would eliminate my Camp Invention work to make time for myself and my interns to assist with research. Ray and I planned to co-author the book.

I packed my best suit and went to New York. During one afternoon, I had scheduled 10-minute pitch interviews with three people who attended the conference: two agents and one editor. First, I chatted with the two agents about Wexner and quickly eliminated their interest once I met with the editor who was from Penguin.

I told this editor about my background, the books I'd written and Ray's work. Then, I pitched the Wexner topic again.

"Everyone needs a personal brand," this editor said. "I've been trying to pitch this topic to my committee at Penguin for several months."

My head started spinning, as she pivoted on my topic.

"I agree with you," I said, regaining my composure. There were only about eight minutes left during this pitch session to get this editor's interest and assure that she would see my follow-up, which I would email the following week.

"Seriously," she said. "People need to get better talking about their own personal skill sets."

"Can you send me your biographies on Monday?" she asked, as the bell rang, signaling the end to our 10-minute meeting.

"Do you want a full book proposal?" I asked, as I stood up in the large room where voices were growing loud with anticipation. More than 50 writers were meeting with editors and agents that day.

"No," she responded. "I'll put together the research that should get this approved by the other editors in-house."

A month later, the last Friday of May, an email arrived from her.

"Congratulations!" she said. "The committee has approved the book. Can you have it ready by September?"

What happens when a big gig comes your way and you're not really prepared for it? Any normal person panics. That's exactly what I did.

"Oh shit" was the subject line in the email that I wrote to Ray. (This is the only time in my professional life that I've ever written an expletive in a subject line.) In addition to my other deadlines, I was committed to writing video scripts and overseeing filming at various Camp Invention locations throughout the following summer.

The phone rang within seconds after sending the email.

"We need to know more about branding," Ray said. We both were flummoxed with the assignment, forgetting our own experience writing about many personal and professional brands.

"Exactly what I was thinking. Do you want to meet at Barnes & Noble to buy books tonight?" I asked. He agreed.

We immediately tackled that topic like we were doing a final exam for a Harvard MBA, reading six or eight books written by branding academics and others over the next week. By then, Ray had spent years writing about Wexner and his creation of some of the top retail brands in the country. I had spent the last 10 years researching and writing about big personal brands for the juvenile biographies. We were well suited to tackle this topic.

Apparently, our editor at Penguin had recognized that before we did.

Wise Words: Why I Write Narrative Nonfiction Books

By Jack El-Hai

A few years after I began freelance writing, I decided I wanted to write books. I wrote three book proposals that drew no interest. It took me 15 years to find a literary agent and come up with a proposal that attracted a publisher.

Since then, I've spent more time authoring books than doing any other kind of writing. I specialize in heavily researched books, mostly on historical topics, that use literary tools – plot, character, setting – to tell completely factual stories. Here's why I love doing it:

- I can pursue, at length, stories that have personal meaning for me. The tales I write about in my books scratch my psychic itches. For example, I've always wondered how I might handle deep and devastating loss. When I wrote **The Lost Brothers**, about three young boys who vanished on their way to play at the park in 1951, I learned how their family has endured seventy years of continuously searching for them.

- Book research always brings surprises. When I became interested in the post-World War II work of U.S. Army psychiatrist Douglas M. Kelley, I tracked down his son. He invited me to visit, and he showed me a dozen boxes never seen outside the Kelley family, full of his father's records documenting his examinations of the top captured German war criminals. My book **The Nazi and the Psychiatrist** resulted.

- I can see my books realized in other media. They have become documentaries, podcasts, and movie and TV series treatments. That's satisfying.

Jack El-Hai is the author of **The Lost Brothers**, **The Nazi and the Psychiatrist, Non-Stop: A Turbulent History of Northwest Airlines, The Lobotomist** *and other books.* The Atlantic, Smithsonian, WIRED, Scientific American Mind, Discover *and* GQ *have published his articles. He's a past president of the American Society of Journalists and Authors.*

⁂

Believe people when they tell you what you are capable of doing. This is now something I teach to other giggers when I mentor them. Some people get that lesson. Others will tell you that it doesn't apply to them, they'll tell you to stop telling them things like that.

Let me say this again, very clearly: *Believe people when they tell you what you are capable of doing.*

I'm repeating that lesson because it's a difficult one to learn. First, you must acknowledge that you may not be the ruler of your own kingdom. Better put, you have to accept that most decisions you'll make about your own career path will be intellectually based. You'll look at the plusses and minuses of various decisions. You'll hyper-analyze every possibility, before you consider changing your career path or even shifting it a bit.

If you're like me, you might even tell people, "Oh, that's not my specialty area" when they encourage you to consider a pathway that is different from the one you're on.

People will see gifts and skills in you that you will not see in yourself. They will ask you to do amazing things. These requests will likely propel your career onto new levels.

Over that following summer, Ray and I spent many weekends writing chapters for the personal branding book in our separate offices at home and passing them to each other for editing and proofing. Somehow, we were able to create a tone that made sense.

Writing the *Complete Idiot's Guide to Branding Yourself* would drastically change the way I thought about myself and my career. It would reveal key words to me that had eluded me for my entire journalistic career.

Here's an important thing to remember about branding yourself. Being transparent and authentic are keys to being successful, no matter your business. To be more transparent with prospective clients, share personal details about your family, your hobbies or your vacations. Ask others about their own interests. These things help people get to know you better. When they get to know you, they develop a personal bond with you. Whether you have a keen eye for design or the quick mind of a scribe, the better they know you the better they will understand what makes you good at what you do. They'll decide they want to work with you because they like your brand.

Recognizing how your clients want to brand themselves and their business is equally important. Once you understand a client's brand, you can better produce the creative materials that they need.

Shortcut to Success:

Brand yourself well for your freelance career and believe people when they tell you what you are capable of doing. Here is a brief branding outline to follow.

1. Write a short paragraph—or elevator pitch—that will explain how you will introduce yourself.

2. Your website should be regularly updated with your elevator pitch and your portfolio of writing samples.

3. Be sure to have a professional photo done that you display on your website, social media sites and in other places, such as book jackets. This photo will represent your professional brand.

4. Your career will constantly evolve. Continually evaluate your specialty niches and determine how you differ from your competition in each of those niches.

5. Prepare for Career Evolution

If you take responsibility for your career, if you know your financial goals, stay open to new possibilities, keep learning about yourself and the world, then you can have a long, successful gig career.

We are living in an age of constant disruption. With huge technological advances and inventions, new job descriptions are created every day. If you are resilient to changes that occur during your professional life, then you are less likely to lose work and lose clients than someone who does not change with the times.

If someone—or several people—ask you to do a job that you haven't done in the past take their questions seriously. Whether you think you are up for the challenge or not, try it. With an open mind and an open heart, many opportunities will come your way. You'll be asked to teach classes, create projects, take trips and any myriad of things that you never expected.

About the time we wrote the branding book, new technology was being launched. Facebook, originally created only as a social network for college students, had opened to the world. Twitter, Pinterest, Instagram, TikTok and many others weren't far behind.

I wrote a chapter in the book about social media and its potential implications for business. Ana, who had met her first college roommate via Facebook, and my interns at the time gave me the encouragement I needed to register onto various social media sites. As I wrote the chapter, I read the users' agreements for the social sites and put much thought into the business applications of social media. "Give examples here!" demanded the copyeditor who was finalizing our book.

I sat in my home office looking at her irritating manuscript notes. "How can I give examples, when this is not yet happening?" I thought.

Finally, I started implementing examples of how various small businesses could use social media to build their brands.

"Imagine a Realtor in a small town," I wrote, thinking of a real estate agent I knew who lived only two blocks away. "She could use social media to show houses listed for sale."

By the time I was finalizing that chapter, President Barack Obama's campaign staff was putting Facebook to work during the 2008 election. Obama's first campaign would become one of the greatest historical lessons about social media's direct impact on U.S. elections.

When the branding book was published in early 2009, requests for speaking engagements began to roll in. I was invited to speak to groups of school superintendents, teachers, even one state department of education. Ohio State University's business school asked for a presentation and, at one point, my resume had to be approved by the Ohio Supreme Court so that I could teach a course to newly licensed female attorneys about social media and the era of branding oneself.

"How would you feel about creating a course focused on social media?" asked the dean at Otterbein's College of Communications in an email in 2011. Apparently, none of the school's full-time faculty wanted to tackle it.

"Sure," I agreed, knowing that the effort I put into creating a course would likely pay off in other ways. There were no social media textbooks at the time, so I decided to create my own lesson plans, based on the social media that existed. Each week, students were required to read the rights and responsibilities of a social media platform: Facebook, Twitter, Instagram, YouTube, Pinterest and others. When they showed up in class, they would take an "open-book" quiz about one of those platforms.

"Please understand that the words that you write on any of these platforms, the photos that you post, will then be owned by the social media company where you post," I told my students, most of whom were engaged with friends on the various social media sites. "Understand that the platforms will own your creative work."

The students in that class were among the first professionals who'd trained during a college course to use social media in the business world. A former student went to work for Nationwide Insurance. Another went to work for Wendy's International. A former intern took a job with Diane von Furstenberg in New York, launching the designer's first social media sites. Another intern worked for Martha Stewart and then helped launch Dr. Oz's television show. Yet another intern launched *Columbus Monthly*'s first social sites.

Somehow, I developed a side-gig around social media expertise. Imagine my surprise when clients began asking me to write LinkedIn bios and such.

My brand work expanded beyond social media, too. The publicity that the book garnered brought queries from additional clients.

The CEO of a small, local hospital requested a meeting. One of the physician founders of the hospital had seen an article about the book in the local newspaper and decided that I was the person who could better help them develop the hospital's brand.

"How did you learn all of this?" asked another physician after listening to my presentation about social media. He was a vascular surgeon who also was part-owner of the hospital.

The lone attorney who was a partner in this development, with whom I'd been out of touch for a few years, was my former client Jim. He called soon, too.

"I need to merge all of my business brands," he said. Jim had a title company, a law office, a real estate management firm and a few other business entities. We worked hard over a period of months to create websites that would fully reveal the entirety of his work.

"Be authentic and transparent," I tell writers and others who attend the workshops I teach. You can't hide any part of your professional life, so just put it out there. Jim was a good student.

James, the publisher, was back in touch, too. By now, he had retired from full-time work as a group publisher and had taken a short-term gig in Texas.

"We need to launch a couple of magazines," he told me. "I'll pay you a per diem rate to visit with my team and talk about a couple of new brands."

The following Tuesday I flew into ridiculously hot Houston where James and his team worked with me to conceptualize two magazines: *Healthy Moms, Healthy Kids* and *Great Backyards*. I was offered lucrative contracts to serve as the freelance editor on both.

All sorts of new brands launch every day. Old brands grow stale. The top marketers in the world continually realign existing brands with new target audiences, depending on the needs of the current customers.

Keeping your professional brand relevant will be key to your gig business. People hire smart people who understand the modern world. It's that requirement— knowing the modern world—that will continually bring new work to you. When disaster or chaos strikes at the national or global level, be ready. Stay relevant by understanding the complexities of the challenges ahead and offer solutions to your clients.

There are many times during your career when opportunities will come your way. Listen to what people ask you to do. Sometimes it will sound like the college dean who asked me to teach the course: I can't think of anyone else better suited for the job than you.

Creative giggers who learn new skills, continually update their portfolios and are always considering new possibilities will have little trouble finding new clients.

Think about the tide, rising and falling all day and all night. Having resilience means you have the ability to ride the waves of the ocean's tide, ebbing and flowing, depending on the needs of the professional world. Don't fight the tide. Flow with it and identify areas where you can make it easier for other people to flow with the current tide of business, too.

I can promise you that your career and your business will change and evolve over time. Be ready for those changes.

Shortcut to Success:

As your career evolves, the economy fluctuates, new inventions are discovered, catastrophes are uncovered, and the world continuously changes. All of this will cause new opportunities to appear. Be resilient and ready to find them.

When Covid-19 was discovered late 2019, there was little content available on the topic. Overnight, it seemed that opportunity expanded exponentially to freelance writers and many other people, especially those in healthcare. Whatever your career path, read the news every day, peruse magazines and trade journals so that you better anticipate upcoming opportunities for your gig business.

6. 50 Ways to Tell a Story

Throughout your career, your hive of professional peers will play a prominent part in your life. As I've mentioned, your colleagues will share job leads. If your work is too busy and you need back-up support, someone you know will likely be looking for a gig. It's a life-long pursuit for those of us with supportive colleagues to learn from and share information with each other as our careers grow and change.

At a Chicago conference for the American Society of Journalists and Authors one year I created a workshop called, "50 Ways to Tell a Story." Together, three dozen writers in the room and I came up with a long list of projects that our clients were asking us to produce. By sharing this information with each other, we confirmed that there was an insatiable demand for gig writers.

Chief among these ways, of course, was creating and updating websites. These writers all had developed websites for themselves, so it was obvious that one skill they had was producing web content. Like me, many had already done so for their clients, too.

I won't bore you by reiterating all 50 ways a writer can find work. What I will share is that various types of social media are also ways people tell stories today. Every time a new social media platform takes off, most recently that was TikTok, gig professionals get more work. Social media has also formed communities for gig writers and editors who can be found, all day long, chatting, collaborating and venting on Facebook, Twitter, Instagram, TikTok, Snapchat and others. If you want to immerse yourself in the gig economy, keep up with social media because it will be quite useful to you as a professional.

That session in Chicago also pointed out that there are three main ways to find gig work if that's what you'd like to do. First, join chat groups on social media sites including Facebook, LinkedIn and others that include other people in your chosen field. Second, attend conferences where you'll meet potential clients and other giggers who can give you support and connect you to clients. Third, make a list of your friends, family and work colleagues then decide who on the list might need your services.

There are many, many ways to tell your story—or to help your clients tell their stories—and they range from creating podcasts and e-blasts to working with traditional media by contributing to editorial content or through advertising. Even the old-school highway billboard remains an important way to connect with certain audiences given that road trips gradually increased during the Covid pandemic.

Spending three hours with a very productive group of writers that day in Chicago inspired me to publish the book that was based on that session. *Content Mar-*

keting: 50 Ways to Tell Your Story took me almost a year to produce but it was well worth the time I spent on it.

Those who were in the room that day knew that the internet consistently demands fresh content. Many writers in ASJA were working on multiple deadlines every day, hired to write blogs for big corporate entities such as Verizon and Costco, companies that were willing to pay a lot of money for quality content.

Shortcut to Success:

Freelancers are asked to do a variety of tasks by their clients. There are at least 50 ways to tell a story in today's world, ranging from social media posts to e-books, from press releases to podcasts, from websites to custom magazines, from blog posts to white papers. Being well versed in these 50 ways to tell each story will give you many more opportunities to partner with your clients as you build your business.

7. Understand Your Gravity Well

Have you ever been asked to speak about a topic that you knew little about? If you're like I am, then you'll understand the angst that involves. I'll spend hours researching and thinking before I speak. Some of my best thinking time is aboard airplanes enroute to my speaking destination.

A few years after the conference that produced 50 Ways, I persuaded a friend, the journalist and author Joanne Cleaver, to chair a third Chicago writers' conference. In turn, she asked me to speak about the "gravity well" during the conference. Joanne is the author of *The Career Lattice: Combat Brain Drain, Improve Company Culture, and Attract Top Talent*. She pays continuous attention to the way professionals build their credentials and create successes.

Here's what my first Google search turned up on the topic.

A gravity well is the field of energy that surrounds a body in space. Think about the sun. Around the sun there is a large field of energy that attracts things to it. The sun's gravity well is what holds the solar system together. A gravity well surrounds the earth, too.

For writers, entrepreneurs and other gig business owners, each of us has a gravity well that attracts projects to us.

But herein lies the challenge.

If your gravity well is full, if it is overburdened with deadlines and other matters, then it just might be that the project that you're supposed to start working on passes by. In part, this may be because you don't even take the time to acknowledge or think about that idea.

The author Elizabeth Gilbert mentions a similar phenomenon in her book *Big Magic: Creative Living Beyond Fear*. Gilbert talks about an early book project that she feels floated by and landed squarely in the lap of another author.

The creative energy that attracts projects toward your gravity well may also be the reason that a project remains in your gravity well—or moves on to another creative soul, as it did in Gilbert's case.

With a room full of nearly 100 writers in Chicago that day, we each examined our own gravity wells. The audience was divided into three groups.

There was a group of successful freelance writers who admitted that their wells were too full. They thought that they were lacking some organizational solutions that would allow them to work more creative projects into their schedules. That group of writers walked to another room where they formed a problem-solving round table to free more time for their preferred projects. They were self-directed folks and needed little help from me because they were surrounded by like minds.

There was another, rather large, group of long-time writers who felt that they had lost focus. Distractions in their lives—ongoing work commitments, family illness and troubled kids—were blocking their gravity wells so that they were unable to pursue projects for which they were passionate. As the group formed a big circle the size of the entire room, they rotated around with each person talking about the project they were driven to pursue. Each made a commitment that this was the day they would begin to better focus.

This group was a serious one and I knew many of the writers in it. As I stopped by the room where they'd decided to meet, one of the writers I knew pressed me for my passion project. At the time, the only thought that came to mind was a project that Ray and I'd often discussed on Saturday mornings when we rode bicycles to get eggs at a nearby breakfast place.

"I want to open a restaurant called Cake for Breakfast," I told the writers in the room that day. Honestly, I think I like the concept of designing a restaurant and baking fabulous cakes for other people to enjoy much more than I like the reality of running a breakfast joint.

Finally, there were the new freelance writers who gathered in our original room. They were still gaining the tools and education required to become successful in their writing careers. To this day, I hope that their early acknowledgement of the gravity well will help them be well-organized in their work and better present during their careers as they keep their eyes open for important opportunities that will advance their work and feed the greater good.

Frankly, by balancing work and passion projects, I hope they can prevent some of the burn-out that so many highly experienced writers face during points in their careers. I know that because 20 years earlier—before I began teaching and working on more creative projects—I was one of those writers grinding out three or four stories a week on the fast track toward burn out.

Shortcut to Success:

Balance your freelance life so that you have a couple days off each week. Try to take 15 minutes in the morning or a couple of hours every night to relax and have fun. Travel and see new things. This down time will rejuvenate your creative spirit and open new possibilities. You'll find that lightbulb moments appear at unexpected times, steering you in fresh directions as your career evolves.

8. Gravity Well Smackdown

Reading Elizabeth Gilbert's book about creative living opened my eyes to another issue. How will you know when there's an idea that you need to grab onto?

Here's what I can tell you. If you are so jolted by an idea that you think of it for days, weeks or maybe even months; if the story starts writing itself in your head before you've had ample time for research; if messages that you get via the universe keep returning in various ways and forms—then it's an idea that you simply must not ignore.

My best example of a gravity well smackdown occurred when I was least expecting it. One evening, Ray and I left our busy work behind to visit a longtime friend, an editor and gentle mentor who was in the hospital. Marty was a gifted editor at a group of weekly newspapers who possessed a keen wit appreciated by all his colleagues. Both Ray and I had worked with him in our early journalism days. By the time we arrived at his room, his wife Nancy had gone home to their two teens and Marty was sleeping peacefully nearby.

We were disappointed that we'd missed Nancy and expected our visit to be a rather short one as Marty rested. Arriving soon after we did was another of the couple's longtime friends who appeared to be close to our own age. We had not previously met.

During our brief introductions—including the fact that Marty had also mentored our own son in journalism—we realized that Kate was the mom of two young children, both of whom she had adopted after they were born addicted to drugs. We didn't talk long, but she answered my questions. We left with the realization that the local neonatal intensive care units were overflowing with children due to the painkiller and opiate epidemic.

A few days after that quiet hospital visit, we learned that Marty had died. We attended his funeral and shared time with Nancy, their children and other mutual friends. Indeed, Marty's life had affected so many. We were sad that one of the best editors we had known was now gone.

My freelance work was busy at the time, but often while driving in my car I'd think of the story Kate had shared with me that day. Eventually, I followed up with her and wrote a magazine article called "Babies Born Addicted to Drugs." After a half dozen visits with Kate and interviews with several pediatricians and nurses, the story was produced revealing a phenomenon that few knew existed. Later, that article won two statewide awards.

I'm still stricken when I think of that quiet evening at the hospital. Soon after that article appeared, the Ohio Attorney General started a campaign that closed many of the pill mills operating throughout the state. I didn't know when I researched that story, though, that I was laying the groundwork for more writing and editing several years later.

More recently, I assigned and edited another story about opioid addiction that made a sad and severe impact on the life of a longtime friend. Alex was the son of one of my first freelance writer friends and, after an accident while serving in the Coast Guard, he became addicted to painkillers. Later, his addiction to other drugs lasted for nearly 10 years. Despite multiple stays in rehab facilities and a clear desire to get clean, he died of a drug overdose on January 1, 2017.

The year 2017 had more overdose drug deaths in the United States than any prior year in this country's history, according to the Centers for Disease Control and Prevention.

I'll never forget Alex's funeral, on a dark and cold January day. Ray held my shoulders as I shivered through the cemetery service. Alex's mother and my friend, the writer Sandra Gurvis, sobbed. A black veil covered her face as she leaned on her adult daughter.

Funerals are always sad and this one was particularly heartbreaking. Alex's lively 4-year-old daughter played quietly throughout the ceremony. Weeks later, Sandra and I cried together for her loss and for her granddaughter, as we ate a quiet dinner and walked a few blocks for ice cream. She told me of the book she was struggling to write about Alex, a book that she hoped would save other lives.

In the ensuing months we'd gather occasionally, as we always had done, for lunch. Eventually, Sandra gathered strength and was able to write easier. When you are a writer, overwhelming sadness or even happiness interferes with your day. A clear head and an even temperament are required to do interviews, take notes and do the creative work that good storytelling requires.

Later that year, I had a contract to launch an annual health magazine. The story of Alex's struggle with addiction could help others, but would his mother want to write it, I wondered. Would it be insensitive to even ask her?

During lunch the following week, Sandra immediately agreed to tackle the topic as I presented it—a rather dry assignment that meant she would write about the science and politics of the raging heroin epidemic. Once her reporting was done, I asked Sandra if she was comfortable weaving her personal experience into the piece.

"I'm writing this as though I'm writing a letter to Alex," she told me, rather excitedly one day in a telephone conversation. "Do you think that will work?"

In the end, Sandra created a compelling narrative about her son's life that made me sob as I edited it and still makes me cry when I read it. I knew Alex as a gifted and joyful little boy, prior to his addiction. His mother's story, which we entitled *Dear Alex,* made his death very real.

What I'd like for you to remember about this chapter is this: You will know when your skills and talent are necessary. There will be no question about it. Don't back away from the challenge. Have the courage to tackle it.

Shortcut to Success:

Watch for signs that forewarn you that your expertise will be needed. Sometimes these assignments or ideas will come when you feel like you don't have the time to do them. When these conflicts arise, you can prioritize the importance of your assignments by determining their stature in the work toward the greater good of mankind.

Part V:

Gain Perspective

1. Dealing with Disruption

Having a flexible career as a freelancer may better set you up for moving to a new city or overcoming an economic crisis. However, a freelance business still requires planning and calculation so that you can keep your cash flowing as your personal world is changing. Any change in the economy or your personal life should motivate you to do a risk assessment for your business regarding the changes you plan to make.

There are other times in your lifetime that you'll just know things. One quiet August day when Ray and I were briefly away from home, a hundred-year-old tree fell across the driveway and blocked us from reentering it.

That's what I call a clear sign that it is time to move. Leaving a house that you love is never easy. In this case, we knew it was time to sell it and a buyer was waiting for the deal to close.

We loved this particular house because it was a big renovation project that we had taken on when Ana was in high school and Justin was already in college.

You might ask, "What does all of this have to do with gig work?" As a freelancer over time, you get quite comfortable disrupting your life and trying something new. I had learned that amazing rewards come to those who take big risks.

This home renovation project, for Ray and me, was a team risk. Together, the two of us spent Ana's junior year in high school working to create our new space—Ray painted walls while Ana and I chose colors, light fixtures, cabinetry and more. Ray and I had a date night to Lowe's where we chose doorknobs.

Justin stopped by after graduating college and stayed for a year working for a local newspaper. It felt as though he stayed just long enough to choose the color of the paint in his room.

"I don't like that green, Mom," he said. "What about blue?"

By that time, Ana had chosen a floral comforter from Pottery Barn and accessories that represented her high school epitome of style. Then, she selected the brightest color of pink in the fabric for the walls in her double-chandeliered and balconied room.

The irony was clear. My nearly adult children— a boy and a girl—had chosen blue and pink for their rooms. With paint still fresh, they each loaded their stuff in their cars and drove across town to move themselves into their new spaces.

We weren't inclined to change the color of their rooms a year later when each ventured out on their own—Ana to college in Boston and Justin to a journalism job at a newspaper on Hilton Head Island.

When you live in a space that feels right, your career—and your lifestyle—will reflect that. You'll feel the pull of a home in a way that is difficult to describe. Writers don't often talk about where they've written their bestsellers, but I'd venture a guess that many were in comfortable places that created good karma. Words or art or music flows from people who are surrounded with good vibes. Researching the ancient art of Feng Shui is one way you can dive a little deeper on how to get good karma flowing in your creative environment.

Ray and I loved that renovated home. Here, we found the time for hosting big dinner parties and cookouts with friends, charity events, quiet evenings eating ice cream or sipping Chardonnay on the grand front porch.

We loved to entertain family and friends at this home. Our former family-focused July Fourth parties evolved into mid-winter slow cooking dinners, an event conceived so that our friends could attend at times after the holidays were long gone, when they were missing their kids and rarely left their homes on Saturday nights due to the frigid temps. The first raucous affair was so well-received that for the second one the following winter, we had to rent extra chairs and establish a dining room in the second-floor commons—a room aptly named because it was the confluence of the attic stairway, the master suite, the main hallway and Ray's home office.

On the day that the tree fell, we knew that our time in the house was about to end.

Without the ties that bind you to a place, as we had during our childrearing years, we now had total freedom. Ray and I were certain there would soon be a new adventure in our lives. The problem was, we didn't know what that phase would look like.

The U.S. economy was in the midst of the Great Recession. Usually, freelancers benefit by getting more jobs when corporations start cutting full-time jobs. That's because full-time workers cost more to businesses who have to pay their health benefits, social security benefits and paid time off. Freelancers get paid for doing the gig but must cover their own social security taxes and healthcare costs. To a gig worker, there is no such thing as paid time off.

What the Great Recession taught freelancers was that two and three years into a bad economy, funds for gig workers also start drying up. At this point in my life, doors were closing as quickly as they were opening. One of my clients, a professor who led a grant project studying the life-long psychological effects on veterans of the Vietnam War, wrapped up his work ending the need for the white papers I'd written.

Publications drastically cut their freelance writing budgets. College administrators feared their endowment funds were drying up, so they honed their annual budgets to eliminate freelance fees for alumni magazines. The list went on. Freelancers who were not resilient during this period of life, who avoided tackling new topics or taking on new clients, did not fare so well.

As time went on, new freelance writing assignments were sparse and book contracts had become nonexistent. Our friends—successful doctors and lawyers and writers and entrepreneurs—had worked hard and done well in their lives. But this financial crunch made many of us cringe. If we could tighten our belts to prepare for our futures, we were all in the process of doing so.

A writer friend near Washington, D.C., reported being upside down on her home. Another rented a high-rise space with her husband in Atlanta, having sold the monolithic house they had refurbished. A third, a lawyer, and his wife, contemplated foreclosure on a home they'd hoped to eventually live in out west. An earlier journalism colleague who had become a nonprofit CEO in the Northeast reported that he had held five management jobs in five years. Budgets of every business and every nonprofit in the country were still being cut as we entered the fourth year of the recession in early 2012.

The PowerPoint I created for the talks I gave about personal branding opened with a slide featuring a surfer on a huge wave. That image was emblematic of my professional life and so many others during this time. We were riding on the uneven waters of the Great Recession, without a clear plan for our future direction.

My work writing about homes is really what prepared me to let go of the past and move into the future. It taught me a lot about people who are resilient.

"Exciting things happen to people who take risks," I reminded myself. The homeowners I had most admired were those not mired in the past, but those who easily packed their bags and moved when the time came to do so.

It's easier to quote someone in an article saying this than to do it.

The air was barely moving the day we moved out of that fabulous big house. It was 95 degrees. There seemed to be no explanation for why that twisted, beautiful, maple tree fell and landed across our driveway.

Finally, Ray received the job offer we suspected would be coming. After many conversations with the company's owners, Ray was offered the position of publisher of a magazine group in Florida.

We were filled with anticipation and excitement as we drove south for this new adventure. For me, I was floating with the tide. Over the next three months, I would fulfill previously arranged contracts to create a student-led campus magazine in Ohio and to consult with a magazine publisher in Oklahoma City.

Beyond that, though, I knew my freelance life was changing. Part of being a good partner is recognizing when the other person has great opportunities. Know that by going with their flow, you will be OK. Things will work out for you.

Shortcut to Success:

Anticipate big opportunities such as moving, having a baby or getting a divorce, and begin preparing in advance for the changes you'll make. This approach will help you determine clients you'll keep, clients you'll leave and ways that you will grow or stabilize your business.

2. New Experiences and Career Detours

There will be detours in your professional life. No matter your age or your professional experiences, those detours always seem to occur. I think it's because we're supposed to learn something along the way.

To grow in life, it's important that you take risks. As my oldest sister revealed to me when I was a naive teen: *No pain, no gain.*

Wise Words: Nourish Your Soul
By Sandra Gurvis

"Stress acts as an accelerator: it will push you either forward or backward, but you choose which direction."—Australian resilience coach Chelsea Erieau

Throughout life, your needs will change. At one time in my life, much of my work was travel writing. That was cool in the sense that I got to take fantastic trips, but the newspapers and magazines I wrote for paid little. Due to a variety of circumstances, including a divorce at age 50, I needed to pivot.

So, I took what little money I had and invested in myself, completing coursework in medical writing and editing. That resulted in a new, enjoyable and relatively stable writing career. My recent move to Florida has resulted in another pivot. I'm writing both fiction and nonfiction books about my new home state.

How do you nourish yourself during times of stress and major change?

Keep your eye on the big picture. What are your long-term goals? Make lists as to how you can achieve them. Periodically revise those lists to remind yourself of your goals.

Break down big tasks into easily achievable nuggets. Rather than being overwhelmed by a 45,000-word book manuscript due in six months, make a chart with goals such as this: Chapter One will be finished by this date, Chapter Two to be finished by that date, etc.

Be proactive. Take classes to hone your skills. Join organizations of interest. Show up at events filled with people doing what you want to do.

Visualize. Podcasts, music and journaling can help lift you up and inspire you.

Sandra Gurvis (www.sandragurvis.com) has written about business, travel, personality profiles, entertainment and health care. The most recent of her 17 books is 111 Places in Columbus that You Must Not Miss *and her upcoming nonfiction book is about the Ringling influence in Sarasota, Florida. She is also at work on a fictional series set in The Villages in Florida.*

Two weeks after arriving in Naples, I put on a black cocktail dress and heels that I rarely wore. The event Ray and I were required to attend due to his new job was called Men and Women of the Year and it is still sponsored by the local magazine in Naples, where he was the publisher.

Standing next to the table where we were assigned at the Ritz-Carlton's Golf Resort, I met the mayor of Naples, a man 15 years older than me. He kept his hand on my lower back for our brief conversation.

"I have a house I think you should look at," he said, knowing we were new to town.

"Where is it?" I responded. "And what's the price?"

"Creighton Road and it $1.2 million," he said.

I laughed and explained that was slightly out of our price range.

A few months later, we made a much lower offer on a Naples house in a gated, golf course community. It was not a dream home, but at least it would be our own.

While I supported Ray in his new endeavor, I soon understood that my gravity well was wide open. New opportunities and new risks were coming my way. We had not yet closed the deal on the Naples' home in early 2013, when I received an urgent message from a publishing CEO with whom I had previously worked. He oversaw the company that had also hired Ray.

The CEO explained that the publisher at *San Antonio Monthly* had suddenly died the evening before while working out on a treadmill. His question: Would it be possible that I fly to Texas to be a stand-in while they searched for a new publisher?

"How long?" was my response.

"Four to six weeks," was his answer.

Less than two weeks later, I was driving down the wrong side of the road in a Kia rental car, in search of the San Antonio magazine office. The damn highways in San Antonio are four lanes wide on each side with two-lane service roads beside them. I made a rule the first week in town that I would never stop by anything that is on the wrong side of the road.

Now, I think that's probably just a good rule for life. Avoid detours. Avoid the wrong side of the road.

I arrived at a squat, brick building and was greeted by a staff still in mourning. Young women quietly showed me my corner office. They had cleared out the former publisher's things and packed them in boxes, preparing to ship them to his wife who lived about three hours away. The staff missed a plastic baggy that had a few fresh crumbs, tucked into a hidden shelf just under the desk. I wondered if this was where the publisher always kept his snacks.

It was an odd day. The former publisher's handwriting loomed on the whiteboard behind me, as he'd marked up plans for 2013. They stayed there for weeks because I didn't have the heart to erase them. Nor did I have a plan to replace it.

A vivacious woman about my own age with strawberry blond hair rushed into my office and commanded me to make a decision about lowering an ad rate for a client who was sitting in the nearby conference room. The sales rep posed two options, then answered herself, and rushed back out the door. I had yet to sit down in the publisher's seat.

The woman apologized for being nervous and abrupt. That is when I realized that life's lessons are rarely apparent, that you learn things along the way that you will eventually need for reference later. You will need to talk about the experience to help someone else. So, you pull it out, dust it off and your mouth is telling a story. Her mother had died just three months earlier, the woman confessed. It had all been a little too much.

I find myself saying: "It's horrible. Someone is there one day, and they are gone the next." I sadly remembered the death of my sister-in-law on Christmas Eve morning a few years ago. She was suffering from cancer and the side-effects of its treatment.

Death is not convenient.

I started a job in a city where I've never been. Ray sent me a text every morning to be sure that I was still alive.

My office became my home. In seven weeks, I slept in five different hotels. I visited the River Walk, Texas Hill Country, got familiar with three women vying for the new publisher's title and, as publisher, hosted a party ranking the most eligible bachelors in town. Three hundred people attended, while I oversaw an overzealous 30-something event planner whose sequined cocktail dress was too short and whose heels were too high.

Due to this San Antonio gig, every week I checked out of a hotel on Thursday and flew back to Naples to attend lavish charity events and parties all weekend with Ray. I had a meltdown when all I could find to wear to a wine fest were black slacks that I pulled, wrinkled, from my suitcase.

At elaborate philanthropic events in Naples, I met fascinating people: the 30-ish man who owns something like 132 McDonald franchises. An older gentleman and his youngish wife spent $300,000 at one charity event buying trips and other stuff to benefit a local children's hospital. People who had retired from work in the C.I.A. Founders of multiple companies, both large and small.

Within a few months, my San Antonio gig was done. About the same time, there was a resignation on the magazine staff in Florida and I was back on the beat of writing about homes and the remarkably interesting people who lived in them.

Shortcut to Success:

Big opportunities will come your way. When they do, create a financial checklist to be sure that your business budget will fare well during this period of time that will limit other gigs in favor of full focus on one job. Unique situations such as my San Antonio job may will bring with it many benefits and rewards. Have the courage to take the leap.

3. Achieving Creative Success

"Do you remember the color of old money?" Helene Gralnick asked her artist husband, Marvin.

They were sitting in a cozy conversation grouping of brown leather club chairs in a gallery-like section of their Southwest Florida home and I was there to interview them about their home. The chairs where they sat were identical to those once used by men while their wives shopped in Chico's stores across the country. Helene and Marvin Gralnick are the founders of Chico's.

That day, at their modern home, the Gralnicks talked briefly about creating the colors that were used in Chico's clothing in the early days of the retail chain they created. Even back in the 1980s, their artistry was apparent. "Old money" was one of the colors they created.

They spoke of tweaking the manufacturing processes in their first Istanbul factories, of exploring that fascinating city—and others—as they traveled the world for the business they founded as a small Sanibel Island shop that grew into a retailing mega-brand.

It wasn't until after this home was built in 2000, its tall white walls looming above, that Marvin started doing art. His murals and other pieces adorned those walls. Early in my visit, Helene offered antioxidant chocolate being made at their recently purchased organic farm in Central America. Broken pieces were served up on a white plate positioned on the long conference room-turned-design table that they'd purchased from Chico's corporate offices a few years ago.

The house where we met was a fit background for the textured wooden furnishings that adorned it, as well as Marvin's artwork. Here and there, nearly everywhere, were political collages and metal sculptures.

The innovative couple who founded and built a public company are liberal, without apology. "The beaches of Sanibel were kind to us," explains Marvin, recalling the days they lived on the island full-time and strolled out their stress in the evenings, walking along sandy beaches. Together, 44 years after meeting and marrying in Mexico, they expressed their concern about the direction of the earth.

That message came across frequently in Marvin's artwork. *Be Kind* is the refrain often repeated. Whether it's meant for people or animals or just, well, the earth.

The Gralnicks are known for the kindness that they displayed as businesses owners. One news story quotes a former employee about Helene signing her business notes with a heart. Funny, that day, in the studio in their house there's a giant metal heart with "love" inscribed across it.

Twice while I was touring Marvin's workshop, Helene touched the heart, and it sprang and jiggled. That's because she and her husband went to an auto junkyard and found the large springs that anchored its base. The jiggling heart seems oddly like their long love affair, with each other and with the art: moving, fluid, yet anchored well in their places in life. The Gralnicks seemed to be each other's best friend, best confidant and, perhaps, best critic.

When they built their home, they told me, they were thinking about the earth and their bodies and the way they could treat all of it with kindness. The white walls of their home were inserted with industrial-sized sliding doorways and large skylight windows at the top, letting in the light, and looking out over the bamboo and ferns and water features—a pool and pond.

It seemed to me that the Gralnicks had followed their youthful passions and had lived the perfect creative lives. They each had been architect, fashion designer, retailer, farmer and parent. They had designed much in their lives, including a restaurant on Sanibel, which they had recently sold.

What stood out was the fact that they had lived authentically, nurturing not only their own creative passions but building a big business that had supported thousands of employees and accommodated millions of customers. Together, they were great believers in creativity.

By that point in life, I had other opportunities to talk with entrepreneurs who had built and sold big businesses. Never once, in fact, did those entrepreneurs encourage others to follow their paths. The work is hard, they know that. The experiences can be grueling. If you are a believer that all people are kind, successful entrepreneurs will set you straight. They'll talk to you about lawyers and lawsuits. They'll draw keen lines between the good in people and the bad in others.

By the time I met the Gralnicks they seemed comfortable being a testament to lives well lived. They traveled among several homes, some in the mountains, others on nearby islands, and that Central American farm. For months after, Marvin Gralnick and I stayed connected via email. I was trying to get Marvin to collaborate on a business book and he was attempting to get me to promote his art. Perhaps the lesson I needed to learn from him was this: Focus on creative energies and don't worry about the rest.

Shortcut to Success:

When you are creating your life's work, kindness should be a main ingredient as it was with Marvin and Helene Gralnick. Be kind to others and work with kind people.

4. You Will Have Bad Days

Even as a successful professional, you will have bad days. Some will seem really bad. The irony I have lived while writing about incredibly amazing homes is worth noting. Even though many people lust after the biggest home in a town, I was never that sort of person.

Don't get me wrong. I like nice things. But so many other things are much more important than having the biggest, most fabulous house.

My first challenge on this particular day was this. I was in Florida but Ana, our daughter, was moving in Maine. The Maine apartment manager where Ana intended to live called me at 9 a.m. on Thursday morning. She had not received the online payment I'd advanced our daughter. Ana would be unable to move in later that morning, she explained. To me, that meant Ana would spend another night or two in a hotel that was charging exorbitant, in-season rates.

As I disconnected, I yelled, loud and strong. Ray tried to run for cover under the auspices of putting on his shoes.

"The damned online form," I complained, secretly glad that he was still at home, and I wasn't yelling into a vacuum. "The online form has held our money but hasn't made the deposit so that Ana can move."

I ranted about the incompetencies of the internet. I raved about computer geeks who can't create a form that makes sense. I rushed from the master bathroom, around the corner from my office, where the offensive form had been filed on my computer the day before.

The naïve, cheerful woman who had just called me, suggested it shouldn't be a problem. "Just refile the payment. You'll get this other deposit back."

I remembered the online warning that deposits don't get returned for at least two weeks.

"You can use a charge card," the 20-something woman advised. Who, in their right mind, would refile a payment for $1,175 without knowing the status of the first one?

Amid my hissy fit, I settled down enough to explain the problem to Ray. Standing stiff and straight, I then communicated to him part of the family schedule this morning. Ana's move was scheduled to begin at 10 a.m. and she needed the apartment key.

"I have an appointment at the same time to preview a house for future publication," I explained. "I need to leave here by 9:15 to be sure I can find it."

Ray cancelled a meeting at work and took a seat at my desk. The minute it was 9 a.m., he called our bank.

I smiled as I drove away.

My tour of the $7 million dollar home that morning was fabulous. Smooth, wooden floors, a glossy long gallery hallway, a broad kitchen with lighted European cabinetry and marble countertops. At the rear of the property was a no-edge swimming pool with what seemed like a lazy river meandering past the master suite. It was reminiscent of the advertisement for the new health club at the college Ana had attended. I remember that the brochure talked extensively about the lazy river.

"This is where I can live," said my tour guide, as we stood in the master suite. He was a rugged craftsman who was showing me around since the homeowner of this huge mansion was out of the country, in the location of his permanent residence.

"He's only like 42 years old," said the man, who was probably 45.

Neither one of us said this: "It must be darn nice to have this as your second home when you're 42 years old."

Perhaps we were both thinking that.

I went back to my office. Ray had just confirmed via phone that, indeed, the apartment had been reserved and Ana's move was underway with the help of a few friends.

I sighed, relieved, before hopping back into my car for my second appointment of the day. This one was about a home I would feature soon, but I'd meet with the designer and her staff at their retail store.

The designer's shop was humming with activity. I'd been here before, and I liked this place. Natural Florida artwork—paintings, odd dried vegetative pieces, sculpture, shells, stones and painted white branches—inspired my creative soul. It all seemed to sparkle, fresh in its design.

A young designer showed me slides of the potential feature home. They were recently taken photographs on a mounted, big screen television above us. "The man bought this place for his wife," she said, unsmiling. She looked at me and added, "I mean we don't have to say that. It was a beach house for her.

"Really, the wife is very elegant," she continued. "She likes nice things. She has good taste in design. She chooses art very carefully. She would bring us a little tiny shell with beautiful, ethereal colors. `This is what I want, can you match this?' she'd say."

"Does she have a design background?" I ask.

"Oh, no," says the designer. "She was a banker's secretary before."

Shortcut to Success:

Everyone has bad days. Family matters and business challenges will constantly occur, no matter your age or your position in life. Expect them, try to have plans in place so that you can deal with them. Finally, and most importantly, forgive yourself when you have a bad day.

5. Learn to Make Soup

It's a simple solution to a lot of problems that you might have in your career. Make soup. The sheer process of heating broth to a boil, chopping vegetables and herbs that will cook in the broth as it boils, will make you feel better. Making soup gives you a sense of accomplishment. Giving some of it to friends deepens that accomplishment.

When the soup cools enough that you can finally sip it off a spoon, you will have forgotten your greatest worry. Sharing a bowl of homemade soup took on a much bigger meaning after my visit to one Naples home.

As a journalist, here's what I can tell you after interviewing thousands of people during my career. There is nothing more delightful than a good conversation with someone who is a kindred spirit.

Myra Janco Daniels answered the door, smiling. Within a few hours, I would find that the charm of this nearly 90-year-old woman was her ability to easily relate to others.

Myra had just announced that she would leave Naples for a home being built in the town of Ave Maria, a newly minted Catholic community surrounding a cathedral-like church built squarely in the Everglades.

Packed full of precious mid-century furnishings and exquisite pieces of art, she had kept her creative space in Naples private for many years. Now she was ready to share it.

By this point in her life, Myra had worked for many years. She was a pioneering woman in advertising, starting her first company in Indiana. At age 38, she broke the glass ceiling to become executive vice president of a large firm in Chicago.

Eventually, she sold the company to a creative director named Draper Daniels, who created the Marlboro Man as one of his campaigns. After his death, Draper Daniels was the model for Don Draper on the "Mad Men" television show.

Myra later moved to Naples and founded the Naples Philharmonic Center for the Arts. When I interviewed her, she had recently been ousted from her position as CEO. The board had decided to bring in a much-younger executive, who promptly persuaded the board to change the name of the building that Myra had raised funds to build. Through our talk that day, Myra showed much grace as she focused on her future.

Inside her home, on walls painted deep, vibrant colors, Myra positioned her collection of prized artworks—among them pieces by Robert Rauschenberg, Frank Stella, Henry Moore, Helen Frankenthaler, Wolf Kahn and more. Her precious furnishings were from designers such as Bruno Paul and others, and in varying styles.

For the seven years that she called this place home, she had expressed her personal creativity here. She never used interior designers, insinuating that would spoil her fun. Instead, her house manager, a designer himself, and she would dicker and collaborate their way through her home design projects—five in the last 17 years, she explained. At least one was in Chicago.

Call it creative tension, but the relationship between the two apparently worked.

"The most creative thing you can do is build your house, arrange your house," Myra told me that day.

She had a similar creative tension with her husband, she explained. She had married Draper Daniels. He had died more than 20 years earlier. But certainly, she says, the two of them "had that thing" that is shared by people who marry their creative match.

Despite her disappointment with "The Phil," she stayed optimistic during our talk. She was focused on fresh philanthropic projects, including a performing arts center and the Mother Teresa Institute. She planned to raise funds so that they could be built at Ave Maria University, she explained.

Myra had hosted numerous gatherings at her Naples home, allowing donors and patrons to enjoy its warm ambiance. One event turned into a sit-down dinner for 75, after starting out as a small dinner party for 20. She had planned to do the cooking, but when the crowd grew, she handed over the recipes to a group of volunteers and played host as guests were seated at tables arranged both indoors and out, around her swimming pool.

The day I visited her home, she shared a story about her $5 million soup. After serving her homemade tomato bisque to a couple of Naples' residents, years ago, she was given a $5 million check. At the time, she was soliciting funds to build The Phil.

Myra Daniels was a portrait in graciousness. She opened her arms and easily shared her love of art and her creative space. Even at a time when many people give up hope in their aging years, Myra continued to focus on the gifts that she could share with the world.

She has lived a life of grace and gratitude.

Shortcut to Success:

Simple acts that show you care about others and that express gratitude will lead you to a life well-lived, both professionally and personally.

6. The Picture is Never Perfect

When you are traveling along the career path where you are meant to be, there will be experiences that will make your head spin. Even if you do not see a direct correlation between your work and the experience that you are offered, embrace it. The answers will eventually be clear.

One morning in Naples I called a Realtor seeking information about Keewaydin Island. The Realtor had just sold a home there to Jim Biden, the brother of then-vice president Joe Biden. It's the small, tropical island off the Gulf coast of Florida where both Bidens, and their families, escaped for a few days of solitude at times.

A few days after I called, the Realtor and I were driven out to Keewaydin on a small boat. There is no other way to get there.

This Realtor had a history with the sandy beaches of Keewaydin and the isolated island situated behind it, called Little Marco. Years before the recession she and her husband, with their two young daughters, left a large home and moved to an 800-square-foot structure on Little Marco.

Keewaydin has grand, sweeping beaches that attract visitors to its vacation houses, but Little Marco is a quieter place. Many times, this Realtor and her daughters would kayak across the waters of Rookery Bay to explore the beaches on Keewaydin. The four people in this family were the only permanent residents on either island.

The woman's daughters knew how to walk around the island's paths, using a stick to clear the way in front—and to scare wild creatures. They learned that if tracks in the sand stopped, they should look up into the trees—a bobcat may be perched on a branch watching over them. They learned that raccoons were mean and that snakes were good because they would eat rats and other varmints.

Living on Little Marco, they closely watched the tides. They experienced nature at its best as they swam in the water off their dock. They knew the time of day that the fish swam in and out. They watched horseshoe crabs and tortoises mate and saw a dolphin give birth. At night, they studied the constellations in the quiet blue sky.

This woman took the opportunity to teach her daughters that nature was circular and that anything they did had a global effect. They knew that tossing a plastic bottle in the water could have a negative effect somewhere in China. We were not in control, they learned, the planet was.

Later, their years on the island were wracked with trying times. Financial and health issues intervened. She divorced, moved back to the mainland, and kicked up a real estate career to support her family.

On that day that she gave me a tour of the islands, the man driving our boat was the person who had discovered her alone, on Little Marco, as she sorted through her family's belongings. This was the first time she had been back since that day.

She hesitated only briefly, before we climbed our way inside her former home. It is a humbling experience when someone shares their innermost thoughts, and this was one of those days. As she quietly gave me a tour of her former home, I could only imagine the images that passed through her mind.

A year later, the same Realtor invited me to join a group of people on a yacht trip out to Keewaydin. She had listed several homes for sale on the island and she wanted to give a tour. I was happy to be invited along for the ride. There were several others who traveled along for the day, a handful of people who were potential buyers, perhaps. We stopped by the various homes of Keewaydin, nibbled on some lunch at one of the homes as we toured it, and sipped Champagne as we walked along the quiet beach.

Eventually, I helped the Realtor write her story for *Gulfshore Life* magazine. This is what she said: "A home is like a womb, a private place where families gather to make and share memories. It's an insular space, private in its perfections and imperfections. Whether it's a small home or an exceptionally large one, it doesn't matter. Neither, alone, can bring happiness. But the memories that are made in a home can bring a lifetime of joy."

Shortcut to Success:

As most storytellers know, a story often reveals itself in layers like peeling back an onion, one skin at a time. Sharing special moments with people along your path is one of the greatest rewards that a creative career will bring you.

7. Have a Sense of Your Physical Self

If you are a writer or another type of professional who spends a lot of time working alone, then you'll understand that sometimes the isolation can be overwhelming. While living in Florida, I had periods of time when this was the case. These were times when my interviews with homeowners were less frequent, and I took on other projects to balance my business.

During one long stretch when I was doing the lonely work of ghostwriting a book for a New York-based businessman, I received an odd message on LinkedIn from a New York placement agency. It went something like this: "A national women's retail brand is looking for a petite fit model near you. We think you might fit that role. Let us know if you're interested."

God knows how they could see from my LinkedIn mug shot that I was the person for whom they were searching. She also gave the range of measurements for hips, waist and bust for which she was searching. (These measurements aren't as small as they may seem.)

After various messages, she encouraged me to meet with designers at the retailer's corporate office. "Why not?" I thought to myself. "It will be a good break from looking at my computer screen."

A quick meeting and measuring session was scheduled for the following week and the small team of women there celebrated when they realized that I—

not one of the much younger women who had showed up—would fit their needs.

In launching a petite line, they wanted to see what needed changed with their clothing designs. Were flowers too big? Were hemline ruffles too huge? Were plunging necklines too low? How did their styles work for women who were shorter than 5-foot, 4-inches tall?

Through the next two years, mainly during weekly fit sessions, I learned a lot about the hundreds of questions that they needed answered regarding every garment I modeled.

One particular question was unusual, emailed to me when I was flying back from a gig project in Austin: "We need your exact measurements today so that we can get a dummy made to use when you are not here. Can you send them to me?"

During a layover in Dallas, I walked into a small, high-end clothing store at the airport. The salesclerk there did my measurements, and I quickly called them into the corporate office.

I signed a contract that says I will never reveal the name of this brand, so I still cannot tell you that. But what I can tell you is that I learned much during that period.

Even though I've always loved the creative chore of putting together outfits, as I matured it was more challenging to find styles that worked. As a professional, some days it was simply easier to wear all black to meetings and appointments.

As a journalist, in fact, I had never considered the idea of stripping down to my undies and having women measure my body while I stood in front of a mirror and cringed at the sight. I'd never considered the advantages of having a few extra pounds on my rear, until the female design director complimented me on the way I filled out the sample slacks.

Throughout my career, my brain had been working extremely hard. In this gig, my brain barely had to work at all. But I learned something about that: I learned how to appreciate and hone my self-image—an image I had never taken the time to contemplate in the decades after I had become a mother at the age of 23.

With mirrors surrounding me for each session, I became more aware of standing straight, with my head up. I learned more about displaying a sense of confidence. I also learned how having a concrete sense of yourself means not only knowing your mind, but also understanding, appreciating and taking care of yourself.

No matter your age, if you are mentally and physically fit, you will be more likely to have the time and energy every day to better contribute to making the world a better place.

Shortcut to Success:

As a writer and a business owner, freelancers need to have confidence that they can get the job done. One way to build confidence in yourself is to be happy with the way you present yourself to other people. A strong and fit mind, as well as a strong and fit body, will show people your inner confidence. Those two things will also help you to work and think well throughout your career.

8. Don't Covet Thy Neighbor

People who have a lot of money—including many of this country's billionaires—are not all good, nor are they all bad.

They are just people. Some are amazingly generous, others are not. Most are smart people who have worked hard and figured out ways to make a lot of money. In some cases, they even seemed surprised that the companies they'd built were worth millions and maybe billions by the time they sold them.

Some people know that their task in life is to help the greater good. But not everyone knows that. Not everyone lives by that mantra. Just because you've earned a lot of money, doesn't mean that you've figured out how to have a decent and generous life.

Successful entrepreneurs are among some of the most competitive people you'll meet. One place you can see those competitive juices flowing between wealthy businessmen and women is in Naples each January, during the annual Naples Winter Winefest, a fundraiser for children's organizations throughout Collier County.

On a Saturday afternoon, hundreds of people will gather to watch a few wealthy folks outbid each other at ridiculously high prices on things like cars, trips and jewelry. Even the wealthiest of the wealthy will strive for the next level of affluence. There is no end to their competitiveness.

It's exhausting to watch, but if you go with the right attitude, you'll have a lot of fun in the process.

Many life lessons have been revealed to me while writing about people and their homes. There are no winners in the competition to own the biggest, most luxurious home. Entrepreneurs who have become big successes keep trying to get the biggest houses. In fact, sometimes they buy whole islands. Still, true happiness seems to elude them.

So, what's my point? Quite simply: don't covet thy neighbor's home.

Secondly, don't covet thy neighbors' careers. Whether you're a new entrepreneur or someone starting out in gig work, stay focused on your own work. Don't covet other people in your field. Don't be jealous of their successes. Whether it's a lucrative book contract or a big prize, the way I look at it is that one win for a creative gigger is one win for all giggers everywhere. Honestly, I've seen too many professional writers get frustrated and stymied because they are ultra-competitive with their fellow writers.

I've also watched too many ambitious people set themselves up for failure by being blinded by the glowing success of billionaires. In Naples, the Port Royal neighborhood is the place where many of these billionaires live. Thus, it's also the place where many people desire to live. It's true that where you live and who you connect with will influence your career, no matter what your pathway may be. But living in the high-end communities in the United States bring along a lot of competition and stress that some people don't realize is there.

Naples' Port Royal neighborhood is the part of town where Chicago and New York advertising icon John Glen Sample—who developed the first radio soap opera—filled in swampy land in the mid-1950s and started selling off lots to people willing to take the risk and buy them.

Today, sprawling beachfront mansions appear to be shellacked in gold against the setting evening sun. Port Royal is a magnet for corporate CEOs and entrepreneurs who have sold big businesses.

Anyone who lives in the neighborhood becomes a member of the Port Royal Club. Only deeded property owners are allowed in; thus, the reason why so many others to strive to own a home there. Think comfy lounges by the pool, beachfront dining, fitness trainers and more. There are some big fish at the Friday evening seafood buffets and that's another reason so many other people covet the idea of living there. You can learn a lot and make some strong connections at a Friday evening buffet.

The neighborhood is an entrepreneur's paradise, where regular gatherings among members of the Port Royal Club reveal rich histories of some of America's best-known companies. Founders of CarMax, Paychex, Arthrex and many less recognized brands (whose names don't involve an X) have homes—and memberships—there. So does Ralph Stayer, who built Johnsonville Sausage after his father founded the small company.

Mix these uber-successful entrepreneurs with former CEOs of Westinghouse, AT&T, Bank of America and others who have retired to the neighborhood and the result: an undeniable brain trust. "That's what makes the dialogue at this club so interesting," one Realtor told me.

The creative class is represented in this part of town, too. The writer Janet Evanovich and her husband, Peter, who've built a fascinating business structure for her success as an author, are joined in the neighborhood by their adult children who have homes there, too.

Local resident and Paychex founder Thomas Golisano—who is married to tennis star Monica Seles—has contributed more than $60 million to children's hospitals in Fort Myers and New York state, among many other philanthropic endeavors. I once interviewed him due to his generous contributions.

At the time we talked, Golisano was ranked #293 on the 2015 Forbes' list of billionaires with an estimated $2.4 billion. He told me that it takes three things to create success: hard work, perseverance and luck.

"If you're not lucky, the other two won't help," he added, laughing. I pictured him, his silver hair glistening in the sun as he wiped his brow after a tennis match with his wife. In reality, he could have been watching the stock news when I called.

"There are a lot of horizons and a lot of opportunities," Golisano said. "You have to work to find them."

Interesting, I thought. That's the same way I feel about a writing career: there are a lot of opportunities but you have to work really hard to find them.

Shortcut to Success:

Most self-made businesspeople understand that there are no real shortcuts to success. Jealousy of others' achievements, however, will often hijack your efforts. Work hard and persevere through challenges to strengthen your stamina for building a strong business. If you are lucky enough to have good connections with successful freelancers or know people who will hire you and refer you to others, then your opportunities will grow.

9. Beware of Predators

It was a warm October afternoon in Naples. The beach house that I was touring was for sale, priced at $29.9 million. The floor was iridescent, made from a glistening, exotic marble and the powder room sink was made of 14-karat gold. From the terrace, I could see the sun lighting up the western sky, reflecting on the infinity-edged swimming pool.

The Realtors who showed me around told me about some private security measures at this home, but I am not supposed to write about the specifics. I can tell you that there was a safe room on its third floor, in case of home invasion, I was told. My mind immediately wandered to dozens of other nefarious reasons the safe room existed.

Wise Words:
When Your Career Chooses you

By Janine Latus

You have no idea what you're training for. I was writing for *O, Parents, Fitness, Woman's Day,* and others, and giving speeches for the Society of American Business Editors and Writers and the National Library Association, the former on how to use storytelling when writing about money and the latter on my adventures as a freelancer.

Then my sister was murdered by her live-in boyfriend, and it took our family a couple of weeks to find her body. My grief and horror overwhelmed me, so I wrote. Pad after legal pad, pouring out my pain. I did it for my own healing, but friends pointed out that I could use my skills to raise awareness about domestic violence and perhaps spare another family from what we went through.

So, I wrote an essay, unfurling her story and introducing readers to the subtle signs of coercive control. The essay ran in *O,* but before that, an editor had said that it needed to be a book, and it needed to explain why women stay.

Writing that book—**If I Am Missing or Dead: A Sister's Story of Love, Murder, and Liberation**—was the hardest thing I'd ever done. I wrote in a coffee shop, surrounded by people. Otherwise, the pain would have left me curled up behind my radiator. The book became an international bestseller and launched me into a speaking career that has taken me around the world, speaking to the U.S. Navy, Major League Baseball and universities, and raising money for domestic violence shelters. I pour

our story out on the stage to help people recognize the signs, escape or help someone else escape, and then thrive. As I said, you never know what you're training for.

Janine Latus is the author of the **If I Am Missing or Dead: A Sister's Story of Love, Murder and Liberation**. *She speaks widely on the spectrum of intimate partner violence, because the idea that what happens in the home stays in the home is getting people killed. She recently served as vice president of ASJA's board of trustees.*

❧

The homeowners were not American, they said. The man of the house was Russian, and his wife is from another Eastern European country. They were moving to their penthouse in Miami where their teenage daughter could focus on her gymnastics training. The Realtors say that they had never seen the man who owns the house. His wife signed all the paperwork. Even though this house sits on a public beach, most people will never find it because it's about a mile away from any public access point.

When I arrived at the house that day, I was greeted in the marble-paved porte-cochere, from which an elegant winding marble-and-stone stairway led to its inner sanctum. Later, one of my tour guides demonstrated a car wash, its sprinkler system buried beneath the heavy concrete arches of the driveway.

Once inside the house, we escaped the hot summer sun and were quickly engulfed in the aged patina of European décor while looking at spectacular views of the Gulf from nearly every space. From its elaborate chandeliers to deep crown moldings to fabulous window dressings, this 12,000-square-foot home counts among the most traditionally elegant in Southwest Florida.

A tiny chapel on its second level was converted to a dressing room for the woman of the house. The inviting lower level offered a workout facility and a private massage room, just steps from the beach.

Of course, you know, the size of your wealth controls where you live. But wealth and the size of a home greatly impacts how people feel about themselves, too. Intense feelings of home and space—or the lack of them—can tear apart marriages and families and test the boundaries of the human beings that you would otherwise consider normal people.

Southwest Florida is often called paradise. This paradise is also an exotic place where black bears and blond Florida panthers roam wild in gated neighborhoods, alligators are caught on camera crossing four lane roads at night, and Burmese pythons that are 18 feet long and as thick as my waist roam the Florida everglades as though they are native inhabitants (they are not).

Paradise is also a place where people sometimes resemble the wild predators that maneuver the terrain, occasionally luring the unsuspecting who live in these large homes, while predators are looking for prey. Success and wealth are magnets that draw all sorts. If you are a successful writer, you'll understand what I mean.

Be aware that where there is success, predators will lurk. As you build your freelance business, be careful about scams, fake clients, those who have no money to pay you, those who will hijack your identity, and others who will attempt to lure you off your path. If you meet someone or hear from someone whose business doesn't sound legit, ignore it and move on with your day. Any business proposition that sounds too good to be true, is likely too good to be true.

In this beautiful and unique geography at the western edge of the Florida Everglades, I wrote about newly built homes that have gutters that spew chrysanthemum oil (to rid the pool terrace of tiny insects), shower areas that resemble elaborate Turkish baths, and wealthy women's closets that are bigger than the nearby cottages of Immokalee's migrant tomato harvesters.

If you look closely at this region, a light shines brightly on America's lopsided class structure: the extravagance of the wealthy weighs heavily against the destituteness found among the local migrant workers.

Yet, wealthy gentlemen who live in Southwest Florida complain that they have become part of a class in which they no longer stand out. "I'm just another rich guy in paradise," two men told me. In their home states, generally in the snow belt of the Midwest and Northeast, their wealth may cause them to stand out from the crowd. In Naples, they really are just another millionaire or billionaire in town.

What does all of this have to do with your freelance career? No matter how successful you are, you should surround yourself with individuals that you trust.

Shortcut to Success:

Beware of predators. As your business gains success, the way others look at you will evolve and change. Protect yourself and protect your assets by being cautious in your business dealings.

Part VI

On Being a Leader

1. Realigning Your Professional Brand

Your career life will be somewhat unpredictable. Just depend on that. The springtime evening seemed to glitter in green as my daughter Ana and I dashed through the rain to greet writer and editor Estelle Erasmus, who would host that evening's 70th Anniversary Gala for ASJA.

Writers, editors and agents trickled into the rooftop space overlooking Central Park as the rain stopped and the sun started to set. Estelle and I gathered the growing crowd to toast the anniversary and talk about upcoming fundraising efforts that would create an online educational hub for writers.

Identifying ASJA's great ability to educate others, board members created the 70th Anniversary Fund that would pay for the technology necessary to create an online hive for those who wanted to build freelance businesses. It was Holly Koenig, the executive director of ASJA, who helped us throw the grand party.

I was ASJA's president by now. Even though it was volunteer work, life was on the fast track working with this busy group of smart board members and committee chairs planning conferences, teaching younger writers how to build businesses, and creating connections for independent writers who live across the United States and Canada.

The energy and productivity of these writers who sat in their home offices around the country was stunning. At one point I surveyed 1,200 ASJA members to discover that some were producing more than 200 articles each year, quietly from their homes. Very few ASJA members regularly work in other spaces.

Two tech writers—both men—informed me in separate conversations that the year before they had each grossed $250,000. I was enthusiastic about the ability of gig writers to put together a lifestyle that meant their earnings could soar.

Wise Words: Freelancing With Perks
By Mary Mihaly

It's one of freelance writing's delicious secrets: there are perks in this business. In fact, they're a necessary evil. If travel writers had to pay their own way to every destination, only tycoons would be travel writers. Sports writers, music reviewers, wine writers, food critics—all are provided whatever they need to get the job done.

Here's how to use (and get) perks in building your freelance business:

- *Get credentials. You won't get season tickets to report on NBA games if you've never covered sports and don't know the names and nuances. If you want to write about wine, certifications from WSET (look it up!), plus a few published pieces, will move you up an editor's list and wine-makers will open their doors to you. In other words, pay your dues.*

- *Network like crazy. That includes attending conferences in your chosen specialty. Three months after I attended my first Wine Bloggers Conference, my bedroom floor was lined with fine wines I was expected to review. If you want to travel, start by writing about your hometown—who would visit there? Have local restaurants or museums made news lately? Attend receptions hosted by your Visitors' Bureau, and don't be a wallflower. Smile. Find writers' groups, attend their gatherings. The work (and perks) will happen.*

- *Be professional! Writing is a profession, and perks—whether they are comped meals, concert or sports tickets, trips or books—are a tool. If you can't complete the assignment without such items, be up-front and ask.*

Mary Mihaly's work has appeared in Reader's Digest, House Beautiful, Robb Report, Playboy, Family Circle *and other national magazines. Her writing specialties include health, travel and wine, and she's earned multiple wine and spirits certifications. She also has written and ghostwritten 20+ books.*

For years, highly productive freelancers in ASJA had been earning $100,000 a year or more. Many had figured out that they could contract with virtual assistants so that menial tasks and proofreading were handled by others, while they focused on the mindful work of taking on clients, interviewing sources and writing articles, blog posts, white papers and more.

A group of dedicated volunteers and I, along with much help from a staff in New York, scheduled conferences in Atlanta, New York, Austin and Chicago to teach others the mysteries of owning a writing business. We encouraged full-time freelancers to spend one day a week marketing their skills to potential new clients and taking care of other business matters such as invoicing and writing proposals.

One committee focused entirely on bringing in potential clients so that conferees could meet them in highly organized 9-minute meetings each day. I understood the importance of those meetings after getting the contract to write the branding book a decade earlier.

Being freelance writers, we knew, meant much more than just writing every day. Those of us who had spent several decades in the business encouraged others to take their business responsibilities seriously. We advised writers to form limited liability companies to protect their assets. Some of our members were authors and attorneys, and they often scheduled sessions to teach freelancers how to better read their contracts before signing them.

Some writers, including myself by now, even form corporations. I always tell writers to talk to their own accountants or attorneys to determine when the time is right for making their business more official by forming a limited liability company or a corporation.

As ASJA president, my volunteer work took hours of my time every day, into the evenings. With thousands of emails and a few conference calls each week, I learned much about relationships during this time, as well as the challenges of organizational management that others had spent their entire careers solving. A lifelong learner, I absorbed every lesson taught by Holly and others at Kellen. It's easy to take for granted the tasks involved in associations in this country, but my admiration for the Kellen executives who worked with ASJA only grew.

It was just after we had toasted the longevity of ASJA when I was approached by an excited young woman who spoke quickly. "Oh my God," said the young woman who walked up to greet me a few minutes later. "Are you the Sherry Beck Paprocki who wrote the book about Katie Couric?"

"Yes," I said, feeling awkward and a bit uncomfortable. Any journalist or writer understands this feeling when they've produced pieces that have been read by thousands. You just aren't sure whether that person will debate a point you've made in a recent article, or whether they will say something much nicer.

"I noticed your name tag when you were speaking," she continued. "You wrote one of my favorite books. When I was a young girl, I wanted to be a newscaster like Katie Couric. My grandmother purchased that book for me since my name was Kate and I read it so many times."

I didn't know how to respond. "Wow," I said. "Thank you. I'm glad you said something."

"When you were speaking, I went out on the balcony and called my mother to ask her to check the spelling of the author of that book," she said. "I can't believe that it is you."

There have been numerous times in my life when people have commented about how my work affected them. No matter what you do in life, compliments about your work will encourage you to continue doing it. When you find out that you have touched someone's life with your writing, it's one of the most gratifying experiences you can have.

Here's why. Research in the last decade has found that being happy will require two things in your life: hedonic happiness and eudaimonic happiness. The first is more short-term. It is based on things such as hearing music, holding a baby, having dinner with friends or watching an enjoyable movie. Eudaimonic happiness is more focused on finding meaningful work, whether that's paid work, a volunteer gig or developing strong social connections.

Affecting peoples' lives with your words is the perfect eudaimonic experience. I have been fortunate to have many more such situations in my writing life.

Perhaps that's why there's so much joy in spending hours doing a gig that you feel is important, even if you're not getting paid for it as was the case with my ASJA leadership role. I knew the organization was affecting not only the writers involved, but the stories written that would have ripple effects on people around the world.

❧

During the same time that I was president for ASJA, Ray was learning about being a cog in a massive corporate journalism organization and that, too, was demanding. We had returned to Columbus when he received a job offer to run a group of magazines back in the city where we had worked for so long. His new bosses also approved an agreement that said we could work together. I was deemed the home and style expert, signing a contract to confirm my duties producing a monthly section and niche publications for the city magazine. Some evenings we both returned to our laptops after dinner to bury our heads in emails and more business from the workday.

One evening, quietly, in my home office I wrote a grant proposal after being alerted to an upcoming deadline. It had been my dream that ASJA's writers collaborate on a project to shine light on a topic of major importance.

I proposed a project to a national nonprofit based in Washington, D.C. that would give grants to writers who published work about people who are struggling with their gender identity. The grant would include writings about LGBTQ community members, their struggle for mental health and other challenges.

To put this issue in context, when I was writing the book about Ellen DeGeneres, I had included a short sidebar on places that gay teens could find help. I was stunned with the statistics that showed that LGBTQ teens had extremely high rates of depression and suicide. In fact, I had recently made an assignment to a freelancer to report on this topic for health magazine we were launching.

I was surprised a few months later to receive notice that ASJA would receive a $35,000 grant to report on this topic. An advisory committee was organized, grants were made to writers, and a teen essay competition was organized. Many articles and essays were published in a variety of magazines and online sites.

The cumulative result of the project was stunning, showing the mental health, homeless and other challenges encountered by people of diverse genders. There is nothing more powerful than being part of an entire group of people who are working toward the greater good.

Shortcut to Success:

Being a leader is not just holding a title. "What's the decision here that suits the greater good of the organization?" I would often ask myself as ASJA's president. Being a leader is about making the right decisions for many more people outside of yourself.

For ASJA, it was about forming a stronger organization for future generations of freelance writers and authors. I understood the awesome power of this organization, whose members produced thousands of articles every year for nearly any publication you can imagine. Thus, some of our decisions for ASJA were rooted in the fact that the executive board agreed on the importance of working toward a greater good for humanity.

2. About Free Speech

The lights were dim as Matthew Galizia walked across the stage at the Sheraton New York Times Square Hotel. As ASJA president, I greeted the 20-something journalist from Malta who was there to accept an award on behalf of his mother.

Daphne Caruana Galizia was being posthumously honored with ASJA's Conscience in Media Award, which calls attention to the dangerous profession of investigative journalism. Daphne had been killed just six months earlier when the car she was driving exploded due to a bomb that had been planted in it. At the podium, Matthew—an investigative journalist and software engineer—solemnly struggled to find the words to talk about his mother's death. He was the first one at the scene of the explosion, which occurred not far from their home.

Matthew's emotions were still raw, and my heart swelled with sympathy for him and his two brothers, who would live the rest of their lives without their mother. Daphne, who died at the age of 53, had been Malta's first investigative journalist and, until recently, its only one. She had been writing since 1987 and was the first person in Malta to have a signed opinion column.

"Daphne Caruana Galizia represents the highest ideals of journalism: Courage, sacrifice and a firm commitment to the truth," said Sally Wendkos Olds, chair of

ASJA's First Amendment Committee in a press release prior to the ceremony. "Her bravery and dedication are especially inspiring to us as fellow independent writers."

It was months earlier when Sally, an ASJA past president, emailed me an important message: "Would I, as ASJA's president, affirm the presentation of this award that had been suggested by the committee she chaired?"

After reading about Daphne's death, I, too, became obsessed with the importance of telling her courageous story. The board agreed with me. Daphne had been threatened numerous times during her work as an independent journalist. She was arrested by the Malta Police Force on two occasions. When they were children, her three sons had received anonymous threats as those in power attempted to intimidate her. The family home was set on fire twice while the children and other family members were inside. "After the second arson, police concluded that the attackers were from the military (the Armed Forces of Malta), but they were never able to make an arrest," said Matthew.

Later, arrests were made regarding Daphne's murder although there seems to still be ongoing discussion regarding why it happened. In early 2021 one suspect pled guilty and was sentenced to 15 years in prison. Despite her death, her legacy lives on.

"Our mother inspired us to stand up for ourselves and for others against abuse, wherever and however it happens," Matthew said. "To not squander our time, but rather to use it to try and make the world better." Daphne's son Andrew is a diplomat and son Paul is an economist. Their father, Peter Caruana Galizia, is a civil lawyer.

Her death caused multiple disruptions to their family life. At the time that Matthew flew to New York to accept the award, he and his brothers lived in fear for their own lives and were not living in Malta, a beautiful independent island nation tucked into the Mediterranean Sea. They tried to convince their father to move away, too.

Sally and I hugged Matthew as he walked off the stage that evening. We, with some others, had invited him to dinner at a restaurant down the street from the hotel following the ceremony. As I made a quick stop in the restroom, I met one of the Galizia family friends—a Brooklyn resident and native of Malta—who was there with her young daughter. The young mother was crying.

"I never thought this would happen in my country," she said.

Daphne's death was one of more than 700 journalists that have been killed over the past decade, according to Reporters without Borders.

Six months after that New York ceremony, journalists around the world were confronted with another high-profile death among the corps. On Oct. 2, 2018,

Jamal Khashoggi, a Saudi Arabian columnist for *The Washington Post*, was killed in the Saudi Consulate of Istanbul. It is reported that he was suffocated, and his body was dismembered with a bone saw by 15 people who were there.

The CIA reportedly believes that Saudi Crown Prince Mohammed bin Salman had ordered the killing, likely because Khashoggi was his outspoken critic. In his first column that appeared in the Post, Khashoggi wrote about the "fear, intimidation, arrests and public shaming of intellectuals and religious leaders who dare to speak their mind."

Around the world, journalists are on the front lines of those who protect free speech. In Malta, Daphne Caruana Galizia tried to protect free speech. Jamal Khashoggi tried to protect it by writing columns in *The Washington Post*, as a known dissenter to the Crown Prince of Saudi Arabia.

Journalists are often the first who take offense when a president or an administration seems to infringe upon rights of the citizens. In the United States, the First Amendment of the U.S. Constitution promises free speech and a free press, as well as the freedom to choose your religion. During his presidency, Donald Trump daily blamed the media. He suggested that Democrats who investigated him should be arrested for treason. He inferred that at least one whistleblower should, perhaps, be punished by a hanging.

As his term came to an end, he threatened Republicans who did not help him find votes to win an election that he had lost, and his fiery speech sparked an insurrection at the U.S. Capitol on January 6, 2021.

While watching the events of that day, I kept thinking of the young woman from Malta who introduced herself to me in the restroom that evening, following the awards presentation. "I never thought this would happen in my country," she said.

Shortcut to Success:

Leadership means having the courage to speak out for what you believe in. As a journalist, I have a clear belief in free speech and a free press. As a leader, you should not hesitate to take a stand on issues of impact.

3. The Truth about Ego

You may have been trained, as I was, to leave your ego behind. If you put too much of "I" into a team project, it is not a good thing for you, or the team involved.

Yet, without ego people may never achieve what they are capable of achieving. The pain and perseverance of creation and discovery takes a dose of ego to drive ideas forward.

Great inventions are not made without failure, I learned during my years affiliated with Camp Invention and listening to the stories told by our great, modern inventors. Big businesses are not built without risk-takers who put everything, including their egos, on the line to make a success.

Ego has a lot to do with the ability to reach deep within ourselves, to accumulate the knowledge and experience required, as we transform our lives into something that has greater meaning. For me, that meant becoming the writer, editor and leader that I had the power to become. It meant discerning what is meaningful in life and what is not.

There are plenty of days I continue to ask myself: "Are you working for the greater good today?"

Here's another thing I feel compelled to share. You will work awfully hard in your life, and you should be pleased with your progress. No one has the right to turn your career and lifetime accomplishments into something negative. Never let anyone take your achievements away from you. When I have a chance to visit Facebook online, I often share that advice with younger writers struggling with issues of self-esteem.

Both important and seemingly inconsequential situations will arise throughout your life that will challenge you. Recently, Ray and I attended a dinner party. The hostess, a woman who has worked her entire life, introduced Ray as a publisher and another well accomplished man in the crowd to dinner guests we had never met. As more guests arrived, she introduced the two men again, emphasizing their career achievements, leaving both me and the other man's wife unintroduced. When her husband pointed out her omission the second time it occurred, she snapped at him.

Grace escaped me that evening, as I looked at Ray and rolled my eyes. He was well aware of my long career being diminished the higher he arose in his own. We had often discussed that. It was an odd mathematical equation for both of us: the more financially successful he had become the less successful I was seen by some. I found that sum total a difficult dilemma to address. I was simply at a loss for words in such situations.

There are big lessons to be learned about earning power over a span of 30 or 40 years. There's nothing more motivational than having fulfilling work, understanding your value and your potential earning power.

Recently, I had a conversation on Facebook with a group of writers. Some women were complaining that their partners were frustrated as they watched their writer spouses' incomes soar.

If you have a partner who is one of those people who seems to have a mental block to his or her on earning power—as well as yours—support that person in his or her journey. Ray did not complain during that period in our lives that my income soared over his. If anything, he's always been a bit envious about the flexibility that I've built into my career.

If you find yourself in a similar situation—watching your own income soar while your partner's income stagnates or even sags—discuss your belief systems about money, about the way that person was reared and their relationship with the dollar. Be your partner's best booster of his or her self-esteem, as well as the ability to earn more income.

Maslow's Pyramid has self-esteem (ego) near the top. This has little to do with the humble brag we have come to know on social media, but much more to do with the ability to become the person that you have the power to be. Your ego can be as quiet or as loud as you want it to be.

Generally, my ego is a quiet one. I don't often talk a lot about my work, but I take great satisfaction in creating projects, hitting deadlines, highlighting the lives of people we feature and encouraging younger profession-als to stretch their creative abilities.

There are times in my life when I push myself hard to be loud. Writing this book may be one of them. I have thought about writing this book for a long time, even at-tempting to convince 30-year-old Ana to be a co-author on a gig-worker's guide as she transitioned into her own gig career in marketing and interior design.

"It's your story, Mom," she told me, refusing to buy into my enthusiasm for the joint project. "You've done it all of these years, so you should write about it."

So, I started thinking about writing this book. And then Justin and his wife, Sarah, brought little Benjamin into our world. I considered how valuable it might be for Benjamin to understand a little bit about my work—just in case he also might want to try the freelance life-style one day. It was during a flight after a speaking gig in New York, when I was about to celebrate my birth-day with Ray and our family in Florida, that I began to outline this book.

Fourteen months after Benjamin's birth, Ana and her husband, Teddy, brought tiny Griffin into our world. I double-downed on my effort to inform future generations about their Gigi's odd career path. Words began to spill out onto these pages. Again, I slid the nearly completed manuscript into my desk drawer.

Then, Sarah gave birth to our first granddaughter, Elizabeth, 14 months after Griffin was born. It was the beginning of the Covid-19 pandemic. The fate of this book—which had set around for about two years in draft form—was sealed. I would publish it.

There is nothing I want more for my children, grandchildren and others who read this than to have careers that they are passionate about, no matter what that career form may take. Being a freelancer has provided me with all the freedoms you can imagine: freedom to write when the mood strikes, freedom to work all night when I wish, freedom to pick and choose topics I cover, the freedom to take a day off, and much more.

But it also includes all the worries of being a small business owner. You must be your company's CEO, CFO, chief operating officer, chief tech officer and chief marketing officer. I don't say this to scare you, but I want to be honest in my assessment. If you have a passion for doing freelance work, you will be able to accomplish all of this and much more.

Starting out your freelance career, you will do all of the above, plus the grunt work involved in your gig. Eventually, you will earn enough money and learn how to parcel out bits and pieces of your work to interns, virtual assistants, accountants, the Best Buy Geek Squad and others to free yourself to pursue the parts of the job that you really enjoy. For me, that generally means being the chief strategist and creative officer that oversees and directs the editorial projects that comprise my business.

Yes, occasionally, I still do massive writing projects—writing this book is one of them. Another was a rather nightmarish literary app project. Over a period of four months, I wrote 38 fiction and nonfiction stories so that two professors at Drexel University could use them as content on a literacy app that they had a grant to build for middle school children. The tight deadlines and emphasis on reading-level technology, made this a challenging project. But it allowed me to revisit the exhilaration of writing for middle schoolers and working on a definitive project that would benefit the greater good.

Put it this way: I know in my soul when I need the salve of a big literary project. Somehow, the right project always seems to come along at the same time.

There are plenty of other motivating factors for me to write this book. It is an important time in the history of journalism. The work of a good investigative reporter can never be undervalued, yet good journalists are losing their jobs every day.

There's not a day that goes by that I don't think about Daphne Galizia's death and Kim's cancer. There's much more investigative work that needs done in this country, including the DERP project on toxic sites that awaits me in our storage unit. I hold my breath every time I see a cancer hotspot reported.

The right to exercise free speech continues to be at risk. As president of ASJA and a representative to the Author's Coalition of America, I frequently signed letters and had discussions with other writers about the First Amendment and practicing the ability to exercise our free speech. These are issues close to my heart.

Shortcut to Success:

As your career progresses, take time to reflect on your successes and your failures. Don't let your ego get in the way as you ask yourself these questions:

- Is it time to adjust my career path?
- Should I take on a leadership role?
- What are the social impacts I hope to make?
- How am I continuing to work for a greater good?

4. Winning Awards

One evening, Ray said that he planned to nominate me for a Folio Award honoring top women in the workplace. Folio is an organization that honors people who contribute largely to the magazine industry in a variety of creative ways: editor, publisher, digital managers and the like.

Here's some background you'll probably need to know. Ray and I have a long history when it comes to winning awards. In the early years of his career, Ray's employer often submitted (and paid for) awards submissions. By the time his tenure as an editor had ended, he had accumulated more than 50 writing and editing awards. They filled a full page, single spaced, on his resume.

Yes, I was probably envious. For me as a freelance writer and editor, I rarely paid the fees necessary to enter writing and journalistic competitions. Somehow, I collected a few awards along the way, but not nearly as many as Ray.

I must confess that this had become a point of contention as our careers had grown. So, it seemed, that Ray was looking to make a big correction. I didn't dissuade him from making the entry—which was indeed a pricy one.

Ray, as you know, has known me since the beginning of my freelance career. He has sat in a front row seat as I've jumped hurdles, had setbacks and dealt with the successes and failures of anyone who has their own business. He understands the resilience I've had in working with a new boss every time I take on a new project. But he also sees the stress created with each new contract.

He's my biggest supporter and I am his. He tells me I can do anything, but that's advice that's questionable when I'm the contract editor hired to parachute into the magazine division that he oversees. With the team there, we launched a successful health publication. Later, I served as the interim editor of the city magazine for three months. When in-house, I walk the tight rope of being the publisher's spouse and a professional editor in my own right. It's a tight rope, believe me.

Perspective always makes a huge difference. Even though it wasn't funny at the time, today Ray and I are able to laugh about our heated argument in an Austin hotel room a few years ago over the fonts selected for a section I was editing for a magazine, which he was temporarily overseeing during a summer that we lived in Naples. In a few months, I'm sure we'll see the humor in a terse conversation we had recently over the tabletop décor I endorsed for a magazine food event. I mean, it's a centerpiece, by God. But as a Style editor I took those matters quite seriously.

Perspective is important.

Ray's nomination for me to Folio was a bit different from other women with careers at big publishing companies, who were nominated for the award. I was the independent producer of niche magazines and other projects. Plus, I was doing some heavy-duty volunteer work as president of ASJA. Ray made the nomination based on both factors. A few months later I was stunned and humbled to learn that I was named among Folio's Top 100 Women in 2018.

That year was a busy one for travel. I tallied my business expenses as I traveled the country to ASJA conferences, other related meetings and awards ceremonies. During the first week in June, I traveled from a conference of the City and Regional Magazine Association in New Orleans to the awards dinner of ASJA's national grant funder in Washington, D.C. to the Folio Awards luncheon in New York. Ray attended all three, the last two only to be by my side.

That's what a good partner does—sometimes he or she simply shows up to be with you.

He was also by my side in Minneapolis when we heard that we'd won the top award for launching a regional, niche magazine in the country. "For a first-time publication, *Columbus Monthly Health* hit it out of the ballpark," said the announcer during the City and Regional Magazine awards. As I carried a heavy plaque back to my table that evening, tears overwhelmed me, and I crumpled back into my chair.

In that moment, it was the humility of working for the greater good that undid me. It seemed so clear. The magazine that won the award included the story about Alex's opioid addiction, as well as a heartfelt article about teenagers struggling with their gender identity. Every writer, graphic designer, editor and advertising representative involved in the creation of this project was responsible for its success.

The greater good had prevailed. I hoped nothing less than the fact that we had saved a few lives by producing the publication.

Shortcut to Success:

Value your work and enter it into competitions. When you win an award, it provides the focus you need to consider the work you are doing and how you are contributing to society. It will allow you to reflect on your purpose. People look up to winners, so don't be humble in claiming your place as a leader. Your win may enable you to speak with others about their own work. It will give you a platform to discuss the greater context of your work as you mentor others.

5. Maintain a Forward Focus

Perseverance is good, and certainly it's a trait that is important in my long-term gig career. Perhaps, by now, I should have been content with awards that I'd won. Still, I persisted.

There was one more thing that I wanted to accomplish. The Folio: 100 awards were coming up, with both men and women competing for a spot. In the era of #metoo, I had something to prove after being named a Folio Top Woman.

Ray and I awaited the results. Indeed, my editorial content work and volunteering to lead a large group of independent writers made sense to the judges. Folio counted me among the top when I was named one of the 100 creative thought leaders for that same year.

Maslow says the top level of the pyramid is the "self actualization" level, which means that you are focused on reaching your full potential. Still, if you are a driven and highly motivated person like I am, you will never feel as though you have done enough.

As I learned from Myra Daniels, one should strive for graciousness and gratitude in whatever you do.

Humility is important, too.

My best advice for you moving forward is to stay optimistic every day. Strive to work in situations that fuel your creative and intellectual fires. Have hope that every day your life and the lives of people around you will improve. Stay focused on serving the greater good of society.

Support your partner and friends and be gentle in your criticism of them. I have not always followed the latter advice, but in retrospect I wish someone would have told me that years ago. I'm sharing it here for you now.

Smart people sometimes expect that everyone else has the same skill set and life's experiences. Let me forewarn you, we do not. Have patience with people in all places—and especially with your team at work and your family.

Just like any inventor or creator, you will make mistakes along the way. I have learned that no matter your experience or number of years working at a craft, there will always be an opportunity to err. Like an inventor who fails at his or her initial attempt, I encourage you to see a mistake as a route to self-improvement. Don't be too hard on yourself, everyone makes mistakes. Just learn from the error and move on.

All careers involve competitive people. Don't always be competing with others for a top prize—or the boss's attention—because in the work of the greater good there is no real prize to earn and the big boss isn't the one in the office next door or on the Zoom call. Be genuine and authentic to yourself and others around you.

Always have hope that you are on the pathway that you are supposed to travel. If you feel your pathway is wrong, look for signs that will help you change that.

Here is some direction: Take time to reach out and talk to others. Listen closely to what they tell you. Watch carefully for a door that is swinging open.

Don't climb over a tree—literally or figuratively—that is blocking your pathway.

Persevere with humility as you emerge as a leader. Understand that you are not leading on your own, but with a team of people who trust that you'll make the right decisions with their help. Have their backs and they will have yours. Have the courage you need to lead through difficult circumstances.

Understand that others are watching and learning from you, too. Encourage and mentor those who will take over the reins behind you, who will move forward to create many more successes.

I can promise you that your career will flourish if you are true to these themes.

"Money is not important to me anymore," I remember Kim, who had recovered from her bone morrow transplant, telling me more than 20 years ago.

"It's more the people who are in my life and the day-to-day relationships that I have."

Shortcut to Success:

Persevering through good and hard times will be part of the work required to allow your career to evolve. Be humble in your pursuits. Celebrate your wins as they come. Refresh your goals every two or three years and rebrand yourself when required.

6. Balancing Spiritual Health

Trust in yourself and your gut feelings. You will inherently know when you need to refresh and relaunch your work life. There are so many times in our lives when we are bone tired—career deadlines are intense, or you have a baby or other family-related challenges. It's always important to find ways to nurture yourself. We know when we need to focus on ourselves and the balance in our lives. Our spiritual, mental and physical health is at risk if we don't heed that warning.

It has taken me nearly my entire career as a writer and many hours of interviewing others to understand how to make the best decisions for myself and my family. Yet, there are many days that I still struggle. I continually read and research information about this topic, and I try to spend time in quiet contemplation, thinking more about the importance of a good work-life balance, our home atmosphere, and how all those things affect our spiritual health and wellbeing.

In March 2020, the world shut-down due to the Covid-19 pandemic. Employees moved home to work remote, schools closed, and many people lost their jobs. Within a year, more than a half million people in the United States died of the coronavirus. I've added this chapter to the book a year after the pandemic began.

This past year has tested the resiliency of every professional out there. In retrospect, we asked ourselves:

How did we get through a year of this chaos? As millions await the vaccine, we continue to contemplate: How do we survive this catastrophe? Finally, we ask: How do we prepare for the future?

That's why I'm finishing this book. I hope it will help you prepare for the future.

At the beginning of the pandemic, I immediately busied myself with a few upcoming deadlines, paying close attention to the ramifications of the virus as it made its way around the world. Ray led his staff into remote work, and they set up systems to do that within 48 hours. As a health editor, I dove deep into the science surrounding Covid and shared information with friends, relatives and colleagues during phone calls and via social media.

I wasn't on a deadline the week that the World Health Organization's announcement of a pandemic closed down workplaces and schools. So, I used the flexibility I had to try to educate others who wanted more information, and I pushed my own editing work into the future.

With a forward focus on taking care of others, Ray and I quickly identified the flexibility in this remote work arrangement. Our off-work hours involved more time taking care of our families. Our four parents were elderly, and a new grandchild was born. I prayed for the health and safety of our family and of the world.

As the months of the pandemic wore on, Ray and I built a kitchen in a condo we had purchased in Florida. We drove to visit our family in Maine. We sent dinner and baskets of food to families who got sick. We tried to tip well when we did dinnertime carry outs. We purchased food regularly at restaurants to help keep them in business.

The economy was crashing, and we tried to help people succeed as much as we possibly could. Doing without water in the kitchen we were renovating was a minor inconvenience given what others were experiencing.

My plans for launching the educational website, Write & Sip, seemed to be continually delayed, despite building a website, recording educational sessions on Zoom, and registering the program's name with the U.S. Patent and Trademarks Office.

The year layered on one crisis after another. Nine months into this pandemic, it seemed clear to me. A rebrand and refresh would be required for every professional in the new, post-Covid world. Following a heated presidential election, a Capitol insurrection and continued debate over race and culture, it seemed as if everyone in society was reassessing.

A year into the pandemic, Ray's father died of a stroke at age 90. Ray and I had just received our first of two vaccine shots. After visiting with his parents on a Friday, we had driven to Maine and settled into a comfortable inn to work remote for two weeks while visiting Ana and her family.

Ray immediately flew home to help his mother get through the final hours of his dad's life. I flew in a few days later, after hitting a deadline that week and embracing the warm comfort offered up by Ana, Teddy and Griffin. This is the first time Ray and I had flown in more than a year. The following weeks were difficult, helping his mother live independently and making a lot of decisions. We took great comfort in communications and help offered by family, friends and colleagues.

Ray and his mother scheduled a tiny, graveside ceremony and I hired someone to livestream the service for the five grandchildren. Ray gave a lovely eulogy, summing up the unique personality of his father. A celebration of life event was planned for the future.

As the days moved forward, I continued to reassess life. I wanted to be more involved in a kinder, gentler society that I hoped was on the horizon. The news announced by President Joe Biden that all Americans would have an opportunity to be vaccinated by July 1, was met with elation.

Everyone I talked to longed for a playbook to get us through 2021. As I finished this book for publication, a Covid crisis struck the preschool that Benjamin attended, and I delayed publication again in favor of spending time with this little guy and his wonderful imagination.

Two early readers of this book, both professionals immersed in busy careers, asked for more information about how to work toward the greater good. That led me to many more hours of deliberation about this pandemic journey and what we may have learned. Conversations with fellow freelancers led to the insertion of their additional words of advice for you here.

I have learned that resilience is key. In a crisis it is important to prioritize and then reprioritize when necessary. Early in the pandemic, I cried hard when I realized that I would be unable to protect anyone from getting Covid-19. I learned that educating people about how to take care of themselves, at home, was primary to my work editing stories about homes and health.

I learned again how much I love science when it unfolds before our eyes. The greatest mysteries are solved with discovery and invention during times like this. I learned to appreciate the beauty of birth, the fullness of life and the finality of death. Again, I recommitted to live fully while I can and to re-emphasize the greater good in whatever I did.

I've added this chapter to help you gain focus on your professional career at any time, but especially following catastrophes. I've tried to create a template for obtaining spiritual health by reordering life's tasks and placing focus where it is needed at difficult times.

As you read this, please keep in mind the two kinds of happiness I mentioned in an earlier chapter: eudaimonic and hedonic. Experts in these topics have found that people are happier if they have higher levels of eudaimonic wellbeing, which comes from having a sense of purpose or service. (Hedonic wellbeing is related to having a good time, such as an evening out with friends.)

Below is a plan to help you prioritize, create balance and focus on the work of the greater good for the future. This exercise should help you get a better sense of purpose from your work and other activities.

Take your time with this activity. It may be days or weeks before you complete it. Get started by answering the questions below to the best of your ability. Then, follow the advice in the key at the end to help gain a better understanding of yourself and your goals.

Exercise:

How to Focus on the Greater Good

1. Let's talk about your family. Check any below that apply to you:

    ❏ I have children.

    ❏ I have a partner or a committed relation-
       ship.

    ❏ I have elderly parents and/or grand-parents.

    ❏ I have an ill relative for whom I'm respon-
       sible.

    ❏ I currently live alone and have few family
       obligations.

2. Now, let's talk about your passions. They may
    or may not be associated with your career path
    at this time. Put an X on any that do not apply.
    Rank those that remain, with #1 being your
    highest priority.

    ❏ Education of others

- ❏ Creating visual art— textiles, jewelry or another sort of visual art
- ❏ Playing a musical instrument
- ❏ Science and innovation
- ❏ Creativity in the sciences and/or math
- ❏ Working on climate challenges
- ❏ Working to help hunger and homelessness
- ❏ Working for democracy and free speech
- ❏ Working in politics, as a volunteer or employee
- ❏ Working on issues related to race and culture
- ❏ Hobbies with automobiles or other methods of transportation
- ❏ Participating in sports
- ❏ Health and fitness
- ❏ Cooking
- ❏ Gardening
- ❏ Nature in general
- ❏ Travel
- ❏ Exercise (bicycling, tennis, golf, swimming, or exercise classes in general)
- ❏ Other _____

3. Can you complete the following sentence with one of the suggestions below? I feel overcommitted on:

❏ Work

❏ Extended family obligations

❏ Volunteer Work

❏ Other _____

Is there a way that you think you can fix the above situation?

_____

_____

_____

Do you participate in any of the following activities to create a sense of balance in your life and to provide spiritual renewal?

❏ Exercise

❏ Yoga or meditation

❏ Walk in nature

❏ Read a book or a magazine (not using a screen)

- ❏ Write three things every morning for which you are grateful. (Or keep a gratitude journal.)

- ❏ See the world through children's eyes by watching them, talking with them and generally enjoying their sense of wonder.

- ❏ Spend time with family and/or friends laughing and having a good time. (Please note doing this without the use of drugs or too much alcohol is the healthiest choice.)

- ❏ Attend religious services or ceremonies

- ❏ I do all the above

- ❏ I do none of the above

Key for Assessing Your Balance, Energy and Drive

Question #1

If you have children under the age of 6 then you'll likely have little free time to devote to yourself to a lot of activities outside of work. Take pride in the fact that rearing children who turn into good and caring adults is a large contribution toward the greater good. Young children mimic things they see in older children and adults. So, every day you're setting an example that a toddler or preschooler can follow. Your work for now is childrearing. But that gives you plenty of time to consider the other questions here as you plan the future.

If you have older children, they will still heavily rely on you to teach them the good morals and ethics necessary to become a contributing member of society. Talk to them about your passions and issues that are important to you. Include them in activities that excite you. For example, take them to a jazz concert, if music is a passion. Take them to a rally for climate change if you are passionate about that issue. Let them see and experience what it is like to devote your energy toward an important cause or activity.

A good partner will be interested in your passions. If you have a partner, share your passions with your partner, and show interest in sharing their passions, too.

If you have elderly or sick relatives that demand some of your time and attention, consider this your current work toward a greater good. Taking care of the sick and elderly in any society is important. Visit them often, talk to them so they can share their lives' stories with you. If you have children, bring them along so that they can see the wonder and enjoyment in children's eyes.

If, at this point in your life, you currently live alone and have few family obligations then perhaps you have time to devote toward improving society.

Question #2

Few people have time in their lives to truly engage in any more than two or three passions at one time. So, anything on this list that you ranked a 4 or higher will probably need to wait for another time in your life for you to engage with it.

For the purpose of this exercise, look at the passion you ranked #1. Here, list three ways that you already are engaged or can engage in that passion. How can you fully commit to being a participant, perhaps gathering with others who share your passion?

1. _____

2. _____

3. _____

How does the above list fit into the fact that you may have 3-4 hours each day to devote to your passion? Do you work in a field that you're passionate about? Whether you work full-time, or not, are there ways that you can incorporate your passions into your day-to-day activities? Can you form a gardening club at work? Can you form a band or a book club with colleagues? Can you organize a group of friends and colleagues around a singular cause, so that you can spend timing together working toward a greater good? If you're retired or don't work at all, use your answers in this key to determine how you will move forward with fulfilling your passion.

Question #3

So often in life, we become overcommitted in a variety of ways, ensnared in family situations and projects that may or may not energize and motivate us. This question asks you for a commitment. First, if you're feeling overwhelmed, identify what is causing that feeling.

Second, take some time—this may involve days and weeks—to do some creative brainstorming with yourself to identify ways that you can eliminate this feeling of being overwhelmed. After you determine your strategy for moving forward, give yourself a deadline.

In my own life, there was a time that I was overcommitted on various volunteer activities that required me to attend meetings, volunteer as a communications chair, create whole events that engaged the community, and other tasks. I loved much of this work and was asked over and over to join boards and get involved in particular activities.

As the years wore on, I made some decisions about limiting my volunteer commitments so that I could fully be present in any given situation. I made a very concrete decision one day while clearing out my office files.

I dedicate one medium-sized drawer to paperwork involving volunteer activities. When that drawer filled to overflowing, I knew I was over committed. The physicality of the drawer filling up really helped me focus on activities that I was passionate about.

Question #4

If you have checked at least three or four items on this list that renew your spirit, good for you! You are well on your way to a balanced life.

If you have checked a box saying that you are doing all the above, then are you happy with this choice? Are there ways that you can spend less time on your own renewal and guide yourself into more work for the greater good?

If you are not yet doing any of the items suggested in this question, pick one and get started! To best contribute to society, you must continually look to renew your energy and refresh your spirit.

Conclusion: Your Plan to Work for the Greater Good

Now that you've identified areas in your life where you must focus, let's move forward with determining how you will proceed. Check the statement that best suits your personal situation and then skip to information in the box at the end.

❏ I plan to wait until my children are older to put more time into pursuing my personal passions and working toward the greater good of society.

❏ My children are older now, so I have some time that I can commit toward my passion. I plan to decide within the next few weeks how I will do that.

❏ I like my work, but I struggle to determine how it serves the greater good.

❏ I have decided to change my career path to focus on work that matches my passions.

❏ I work in a field that I'm passionate about and I continually feel as though I'm working toward the greater good. However, my income suffers because I work in this field.

❏ I have it figured out. I feel as though my life and work are balanced. I have risen to a level in my work that I'm well paid while I mentor and motivate a team of others. We all have a sense of purpose in our work, and we continually feel as though we are working toward the greater good of society.

❏ I have struck balance in my life. Even though I struggle to determine how my career serves the greater good, the money I earn is exceptionally good. I own or work for a company or nonprofit that has high morals and strong values. I make regular contributions of time and donate money to causes that reflect my passions. I organize events or serve on boards of nonprofits that work in these fields. I also seek other ways to engage with those who work on the cause. I continually express gratitude to them for doing so.

After you've checked the statement that best describes your situation, contemplate the others that follow. They will provide clues to you about the path you may decide to follow in the future. There is not one clear answer about working toward the greater good of society and how to go about that. In the above exercise, for example, checking any box will help you prioritize your current work in terms of the greater good.

Join Me at the Following Places

SherryBeckPaprocki.com

FreelanceFancy.com

WriteandSip.com

Rsrock.media

Find Your Hive of Peers

When you become a freelancer, it's much easier if you have a group of experienced professionals available who can answer your questions and discuss ideas with you. Following are some places where you can find support.

1. **The American Society of Journalists and Authors** (ASJA.org)

2. **Garden Writers** GardenComm | Garden Communicators International | New York, NY (GardenComm.org)

3. **Society of American Travel Writers** (SATW.org)

4. **American Medical Writers Association** (AMWA.org)

5. **Association of Healthcare Journalists** (healthjournalism.org)

6. **Society of Professional Journalists** Society of Professional Journalists - Improving and protecting journalism since 1909 (spj.org)

7. **Society of Environmental Journalists** (SEJ.org)

8. **Freelance Success**
    Freelance Success: The ultimate resource for estab-
    lished, professional nonfiction writers
    (FreelanceSuccess.com)

9. **Textbook and Academic Authors Association**
    (taaonline.net)

10. **Society of Children's Book Authors and Illustrations**
    (SCBWI.org)

11. **Authors Guild (for book authors)**
    (AuthorsGuild.org)

Additional books by Sherry Beck Paprocki

Content Marketing: 50 Ways to Tell Your Story (R.S. Rock Media, Inc. 2015)

Women of Achievement: Anita Roddick (Juvenile nonfiction, Chelsea House, 2010)

Women of Achievement: Princess Diana (Juvenile nonfiction, Chelsea House, 2009)

The Complete Idiot's Guide to Branding Yourself (Alpha/Penguin, 2009)

Women of Achievement: Martha Stewart (Juvenile nonfiction, Chelsea House, 2009)

Women of Achievement: Ellen DeGeneres (Juvenile nonfiction, Chelsea House, January 2009)

Oprah Winfrey: Legacy Edition (Juvenile nonfiction, Chelsea House, 2006)

Bob Marley: Legacy Edition (Juvenile nonfiction, Chelsea House, 2006)

World Leaders: Vicente Fox (Juvenile nonfiction, Chelsea House, 2002)

Women of Achievement: Katie Couric (Juvenile, Chelsea House, 2001)

Women Who Win: Michelle Kwan (Juvenile, Chelsea House, 2001)

CPSIA information can be obtained
at www.ICGtesting.com
Printed in the USA
BVHW041647021221
623089BV00020B/732

9 780996 306522